foreword

Research and technological development are determining factors in the competitiveness of the European economies and their position on world markets. European research has achieved significant breakthroughs this century, and its variety, richness and quality are plain to see. Nevertheless, there is a reduction in innovativeness in some of those areas which will determine the winners and losers of the years to come.

The importance of scientific and technological cooperation to the single market is well known, even if it is not yet a reality in all areas. Too often, researchers find themselves confronted by barriers of culture, tradition, or bureaucracy, when they, of all professions, should be free to communicate, cooperate and exchange ideas.

The European Union, with the mandate of the Treaty of Maastricht, has important tasks to accomplish in the area of RTD: cooperation, coordination, and common strategies are on the agenda. Essential conditions for this are more transparency, and better communication between partners from 15 different research environments. In recent years, there has been much progress in this direction. Today, the European Union is, if not the only one, at least the most important platform for European cooperation. The Fourth Framework Programme is unique in Europe, and must bring about the creation of a genuine European technological community.

During my first year as a member of the European Commission, I have taken a number of initiatives directed towards increased transparency and focusing of resources, most notably through the creation of Task Forces in several key technological sectors: the car of tomorrow, the train of the future, new generation aircraft, transport intermodality, multimedia educational software, vaccines and viral diseases, and maritime systems of the future. These are research subjects which will not only make a vital contribution to the competitiveness of European industry in this age of globalisation, but also be of interest and concern for the citizens of Europe.

This is why I, together with my fellow commissioners, consider it essential to improve the transparency and visibility of research and technology policy. At a time when technological developments affect virtually all human activities, I consider information on Community research to be a contribution to democracy.

And that's what this guide is about. Originally intended for the ever-increasing numbers of participants in Community research programmes, it serves equally well to answer, in clear and simple terms, the questions in everyone's mind as to the value and success of the European Union's activities in this area which is so important for our future.

Edith Cresson

Commissioner responsible *for Research, Education and Training*

introduction

Is it worth taking the Brussels road?
For what kind of projects are the EC programmes the most appropriate?
What are the chances of my project being accepted?
What's the best way to go about things?
Where can I get the preliminary information I need?
Who can provide me with advice and support?
How do I find a partner?
What conditions must I fulfil, and will the outcome be worth the effort?

These are the questions that concern not only potential applicants with no previous experience of EC research, but very often also experienced partners, who are trying to find their way through the wealth of technical and legal information available.

The earlier editions of this guide, produced in the early '90s, helped improve the information on and understanding of Community research programmes considerably. By avoiding legal and technical EC jargon the guide became a standard tool both for those who had already participated in research programmes and for newcomers. The guide is designed to provide:

► a descriptive outline - intelligible to all, including the layman - of the problems associated with information, obtaining advice, submission of applications, financing, etc.

► a succinct outline of the content and procedures of each programme, in the form of "fact sheets"

► practical hints for interested parties, ranging from the search for partners to the completion of a potentially successful project proposal.

The popularity of the guide has exceeded all expectations, and shows that there was a considerable gap to be closed.

This new edition consists primarily of a presentation of the Fourth Framework Programme. The presentation of the research and other related programmes has been improved and extended. In addition, Part 1 (RTD policy) and Part 3 (research contracts) have been completely rewritten in order to take account of developments since the end of 1992, and particularly the steps that have been taken to render Community support for research more transparent and rational, such as the new, simpler model contract, and the setting up of the industry-research Task Forces.

contents

Part 2
From the idea to the project

PART 3
What Community research contracts cover

PART 4
An outline of the programmes of the Fourth Framework Programme

Annex

PART 5
Related Programmes outside the Framework Programme

RESEARCH AND TECHNOLOGICAL DEVELOPMENT

AFTER MAASTRICHT

- FRESH SCOPE

FOR NEW TASKS

PART ①

1 | COMMUNITY RTD-TODAY AND TOMORROW

In 1995, for various reasons research and technology in the European Union
are more to the forefront than ever before:

- In recent years research and technological development have taken on a
  new meaning. Our lives in all sectors of the economy, society and the private sphere are being influenced more and more by key developments in
  such areas as information and communication technologies, material sciences and biotechnology. Technological developments continue to reach
  new heights, technical knowledge doubles within a few years, research
  and development costs are increasing dramatically, and the *globalization*
  of markets is already a reality in high-tech sectors.
- What this means is that the European dimension in research and technology is now vital for the European economy. There is now no country or
  sector of the economy where the need for a research and technology policy at EU level is questioned. This is evident from the key role played by
  technology policy in the Commission's *White Paper on Growth,
  Competitiveness and Employment* published in December 1993. The fact
  that investment in research and technological development determines
  economic growth, jobs and the position of European industry in tomorrow's world markets is now beyond dispute.
- At the beginning of 1995, RTD policy in the EU reached an important turn-
  ing point with the smooth changeover from the third to the Fourth
  Framework Programme. By the beginning of December 1994, the Council
  of Ministers had adopted all the specific programmes, the first calls for
  proposals being published soon after, and the Fourth Framework
  Programme effectively entered into force in January 1995.
- This transition was achieved in record time, despite the fact that the decision-making process was the first practical application of the new (and
  somewhat more complex) decision-making process established by the

Maastricht treaty. The deciding factor was the conviction that the structural problems of European countries could only be overcome by means of a substantial input at technological level. For we now know that the diminishing competitiveness of European industry is not just a matter of companies' excessive cost structures, but is also due to a loss of momentum in innovation and technology transfer in European industry.

There is therefore a clear link between competitiveness, employment and technological performance. The balance of patents in the Member States makes this absolutely clear, as does the relative technology component of Member States' exports.

However, the Community is not trying to monopolise European-level research and technology. This would be neither wise nor indeed feasible with the resources available. Despite considerable growth in the Community's research budget, it is still relatively limited at about 4% of public expenditure on research and development in the Member States, or just 2% if private and public moneys are lumped together. There are also a number of multilateral projects which involve European cooperation and are run outside the framework of Community research. Some of these, e.g. AIRBUS, ARIANE, EUREKA, have been very successful. Altogether they bring the European proportion of all research expenditure up to about 13%. Thus research and development are still primarily the affair of the Member States and their industries. This is only to be expected, and is laid down by the principle of subsidiarity in the Maastricht Treaty: the European Union takes action only where action at a lower level is less conducive to achieving a particular objective.

Today, more and more scientific problems in the economy, society, environment and medicine are proving impossible to solve within national boundaries. Thus, the principle of subsidiarity leaves a far greater need for action at a European level than the Community can handle.

The main thrust of RTD policy in the Community is still the maintenance and improvement of industrial competitiveness. Nevertheless, the Community cannot restrict itself to a definition constructed solely in terms of business economics. Competitiveness today is determined not only by companies' cost structures, productivity and profitability, but also by a variety of factors which make up our living and business conditions: environment and quality of life, health, safety, social environment and the ability not only to solve problems, but to prevent them from occurring.

At a European level in particular, therefore, the entire spectrum of today's living conditions and opportunities must be taken into account if, on the threshold of the twenty-first century, the Community is to play the role expected of it in Europe and in the world.

Trends in RTD expenditures

as a percentage of total Community expenditures

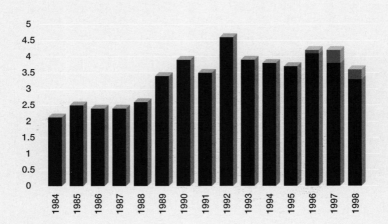

■ Commitments

■ Reserve of ECU 700 million

2 | THE MEANS OF COOPERATION

The main political instrument of Community research is the framework programme, a plan devised by the Commission in close cooperation with the
worlds of science, economics and politics, which provides all the essential
elements (basic legal and administrative conditions, scientific and technical
targets and contents, and above all financial resources) for a period of five
years and thus makes for a medium- to long-term strategy. Proof of this
broad political commitment is borne out by the fact that the decision on the
framework programme in the Council of Ministers was unanimous.

How does it work?

1. **International partnerships:** Support will be given to research projects involving international cooperation between industry, universities and research laboratories with at least two parties involved from different Member States. Although industry as a whole plays a major part in Community programmes, small businesses have some catching up to do.

2. **Selection:** Research projects are not funded according to national quotas as in the Social or Structural (regional) Funds. The main criterion for the selection of research projects is scientific and technical quality. This is followed by economic criteria such as effects on growth and competitiveness, the job market or environmental conditions.

   There can thus be no a *priori* claims to Community research funding. It would also be wrong for any participating country to expect a balance between its payments (into the research budget) and returns (in the form of project funding).

   This type of *juste retour* thinking is out of place in research policy, and by the same token there can be no legal or political claims whatsoever to funding.

3. **Participation incentive:** Consequently, funding is not in the final analysis a subsidy but rather a kind of prize: only the most convincing proposals in terms of scientific excellence, innovation and European added value have a chance. Research funding is thus based more on competition than other financial instruments, and it is advisable to realise even at the preparatory stage that the selection process is very demanding, and that often only a very limited number of even first-rate applications are successful. Above all, potential applicants should not let themselves be governed solely by financial considerations. More important are the long-term effects of cooperation, such as the establishment of links and partnerships, innovation and the building of networks, which in the end often have a far greater value to the research partners than an individual project.

4. **Technological focus:** In principle only basic research and pre-competitive projects are eligible for funding at Community level; the closer a project is to the market the lower its chances will be. In the Commission's view, product development and market entry must remain the task of private industry.

Nevertheless, in times of recession and scarce funds, a trend towards more market proximity and application orientation can also be justified in Community research.

5. **Direct contact:** Research cooperation contracts are prepared and concluded directly between the Commission and the applicants, thus dispensing with administrative intermediate stages at country and regional level. This places greater demands on the willingness of the interested parties to cultivate contacts on the spot and to obtain information at source. In an area with 370 million people this cannot be the sole responsibility of the Commission. In the interests of everyone involved, information should not just be provided, but also sought out. In this respect the Commission is a valuable source of a wide range of informational material.

3 | THE FOURTH FRAMEWORK PROGRAMME

The operational phase of the Fourth Framework Programme for research and technological development began on 15 December 1994 with the first calls for proposals. The framework programme runs until the end of 1998 and had an original budget of ECU 12.3 billion (about £10 billion), now increased by ECU 800 million to reflect the accession of the new member states (Austria, Finland, Sweden).

The main aims of research policy in the Fourth Framework Programme are as follows:

1 **Support for the scientific and technical bases** of European industry to help it compete in key technological areas with its rivals on the world markets, especially the USA and Japan.

2 **Coordination** of research policy between the Member States and the Community.

3 **Utilisation and dissemination** of research results to overcome European weaknesses in technology transfer, in particular among small businesses.

4 **Technological support** for the whole of EU policy (such as transport, environmental and social policy) in order to boost the technological dimension of the European internal market.

Fourth Framework Programme (1994 to 1998)

1. Research, technological development and demonstration programmes

1.	Information technologies	2035
2.	Telematics applications	898
3.	Advanced communication technologies and services	671
4.	Industrial and materials technologies	1722
5.	Standards, measurements and testing	184
6.	Environment and climate	566.5
7.	Marine science and technology	243
8.	Biotechnology	588
9.	Biomedicine and health	358
10.	Agriculture and fisheries	646.5
11.	Non-nuclear energy	1030
12.	Nuclear fission safety	170.5
13.	Controlled thermonuclear fusion	846
14.	Transport	256
15.	Targeted socio-economic research	112
16.	Direct measures (Joint Research Centre)	1094.5

2.	**Cooperation with third countries and international organisations**	575
3.	**Dissemination and optimization of results**	312
4.	**Training and mobility of researchers**	792
	Total	**13100**

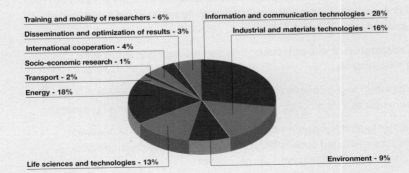

Training and mobility of researchers - 6%
Dissemination and optimization of results - 3%
International cooperation - 4%
Socio-economic research - 1%
Transport - 2%
Energy - 18%
Information and communication technologies - 28%
Industrial and materials technologies - 16%
Life sciences and technologies - 13%
Environment - 9%

The Fourth Framework Programme also emphasises a number of new points

The main strategic goals are as follows:

▸ Creation of high-level **infrastructures** in information technology, communications, transport and energy. These *European networks* are designed to be the technological dimension of the European internal market.

▸ **Greater competitiveness** in industrial technologies and their compatibility with quality of life, environmental protection and safety; smart, *clean* production technologies.

▸ **Environmental protection** as an aid to competitiveness in industry-linked programmes; inclusion of environmental criteria in all areas.

▸ Systematic **dissemination and utilisation** of research results, in particular for small businesses.

▸ **Coordination** of member states' R&D policies with Community research policy.

The main new features of the Fourth Framework Programme are as follows

▸ For the first time all the research work of the European Commission, which hitherto had been spread over the various Directorates-General (e.g. agriculture, industry, environment, etc.), now comes under the framework programme.

▸ Similarly, the various international cooperation projects are grouped together for the first time in an independent sphere of action divided into the various geographical areas of central and eastern Europe, developing countries and non-European industrialised countries.

▸ The programme for *Dissemination and optimization of results* has been expanded with the allocation of a much larger budget. Under this programme, the establishment of a new Europe-wide network of relay centres is of great interest to potential candidates for RTD programmes. These centres often go beyond their main task as vehicles for technology transfer and also provide information, consultancy and assistance for Community projects.

▸ Promotion of training and mobility of researchers with the inclusion in particular of interested parties from peripheral and disadvantaged regions to help cohesion and to offset the technological north-south divide within the Community.

▶ Development of synergy between research and structural policies, in particular with regional policy, which are far more generously funded and above all provide scope for institutional funding. In view of the divide in technological infrastructure within the EU this is a highly promising option which will be systematically pursued in the years ahead through cooperation with the Member States.

The Task Forces

The most important innovation is the establishment of Task Forces in several key technological areas, whereby research activities which have hitherto been fragmented can be coordinated and implemented in a focused way. This will take place first of all within the Commission, and subsequently between the Commission and the Member States. In this context, systematic consultation with the interested industrial sectors is of major importance. Of course, it's not a question of relieving industry of its responsibilities, or its right to entrepreneurial autonomy, nor its right to establish its own priorities. All of this, given our free-market economy, must naturally remain the business of industry. On the other hand, we have seen time and again that the Commission can play a catalytic role in areas of major economic and social importance.

In this case, the objective is to ensure a level of transparency, synergy and coordination that will allow an optimal allocation of resources in those areas which directly influence competitiveness, job-creation, and growth. In addition, it is important to concentrate on those projects which respond to the concerns of the general public, in order to demonstrate that Community research benefits them directly. With this in mind, in April 1995 the Commission set up task forces in six different areas, adding a seventh towards the end the year. Their objectives: to carry out an in-depth analysis of the technological, industrial and social aspects of sectors with high-tech potential such as transportation, education, and communication. This focus on topics of current concern has led to the identification of the following areas:

▸ Closer links between research and education policy, which have so far developed more or less independently of one another, but show a certain amount of potential for synergy.

▸ the car of tomorrow
▸ the train and rail systems of the future
▸ new generation aircraft
▸ transport intermodality and interoperability
▸ educational software and multimedia
▸ vaccines and viral diseases
▸ maritime systems of the future

This approach must take into account the interests and needs of SMEs just as much as those of larger industrial concerns; neither must the geographic and industrial diversity of the EU be ignored. In this way, a new impetus will be given to the strengthening of relations between research and industry, relations which are still under-developed in comparison with our major international competitors. In addition, on the basis of economic, scientific and technical analysis of the results, it is planned to define clusters of concrete projects.

The various task forces are run by those Commission directors (department heads) responsible for the different areas of research; their names and contact details are listed at the end of this brochure.

At an operational level, it should be noted that, within the Fourth Framework Programme, the task forces will concentrate mainly on analysis and conceptual work, with concrete applications coming later, probably during the Fifth Framework Programme. Nevertheless, for those working in the areas covered by the task forces, it's certainly well worth while finding out more about their work, even at this stage.

Financial resources

The budget for the Fourth Framework Programme was initially ECU 12.3 billion (approx. £10 billion) for the years 1995-98, now increased by ECU 800 million following the accession of the new member states; whether or not to add a second tranche of ECU 700 million will be decided by the end of June 1996.

However, this seemingly impressive allocation, compared with the ECU 6.7 billion of the third framework programme, is by no means double the funds in real terms, given that the Fourth Framework Programme now covers all the research work that was previously spread over many individual sectors (e.g. energy, steel, agriculture, environment). On the other hand, bringing all research under the umbrella of the framework programme is certainly a step in the right direction towards transparency, as it is now much easier to obtain an overall picture of the research activities funded by the European Commission

Taking all these factors into account, the annual growth rate of financial resources in the Fourth Framework Programme amounts to just under 5%-clearly much lower than in the third programme but by no means inconsiderable given the general climate of financial restrictions on public research.

With constantly increasing expectations from industry and science, this means that the limited funds for Community research must be used even more prudently, and with precise objectives in mind.

The practical consequence for both the traditional project partner and the newcomer is that each will have to decide even more carefully than before whether, for a given project, Community research really is the right track. The principle of subsidiarity, a key element of European policy since the Maastricht Treaty, must be applied systematically and seriously, not least in the area of research and development. With this in mind, prospective research partners would be well advised to check their proposal very carefully against the corollary pre-condition of European added value before making an application, if unnecessary investment in time and money is to be avoided.

Better programme management

At the same time as preparing the Fourth Framework Programme the Commission took a number of concrete steps to improve programme transparency and management which are of particular practical importance.

These include:
- standardisation and simplification of application forms (shortened to six pages)
- introduction of four, annual fixed dates for calls for proposals (15 March, 15 June, 15 September, 15 December)
- rotating terms of office for expert committees so that no national expert spends more than three years on any one committee. This should help with the independence and objectivity of the work of the assessment committees. In addition, there will be systematic information on the selection of experts, publication of selection criteria for projects, etc.

Above all the Commission has spared no expense over the last two years to improve information and access to what the programme has to offer: from the various manuals and guides for applicants, which have become the trade mark of Community research, to the systematic supply of the various information points (Euro Info Centres, Innovation Relay Centres) with information material and packages, and the new, free, bi-monthly *RTD Info* newsletter which provides a quick, easy-to-read overview of programme development, calls for proposals, contact persons, conferences, publications, etc.

The four areas of activity in detail

The second (1987-91) and third (1990-95) framework programmes already covered practically the entire spectrum of modern research in natural and engineering sciences, from the industry-related fields of information, communication and materials research, to biotechnology, energy, medical research and the environment.

The Fourth Framework Programme, while adding some new areas of research, picks up the main topics of the third framework programme. At 87% of the budget, these take up the lion's share of financial resources, and provide the continuity and security of long-term planning, which are an essential feature of Community research.

The new framework programme is
divided into four major areas of activity.

Activity 1

| Research, technological development
and demonstration programmes

By and large this covers research subjects from the third framework programme, almost all of which are included, albeit sometimes under different
guises. In content terms, however, the Fourth Framework Programme also
focuses on new priorities in these traditional programmes, as can be seen
from the diagram below.

The following programmes, for example, are better funded than
their predecessors not only in absolute terms but also relatively:

- telematics applications
- industrial technologies and new materials
- environmental research
- life sciences and health research
- energy research

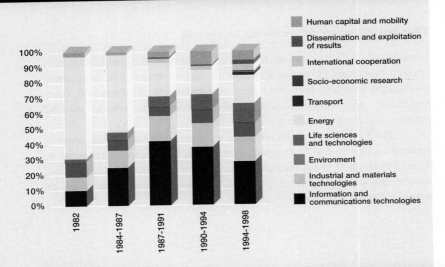

Changes in RDT priorities between
framework programmes

Legend:
- Human capital and mobility
- Dissemination and exploitation of results
- International cooperation
- Socio-economic research
- Transport
- Energy
- Life sciences and technologies
- Environment
- Industrial and materials technologies
- Information and communications technologies

Years: 1982, 1984-1987, 1987-1991, 1990-1994, 1994-1998

This funding is partly at the cost of information and communication technologies which in the second and third framework programmes consumed about 40% of the resources. Nevertheless, these programmes still dwarf most of the others in absolute terms, with funding of ECU 3.6 billion or 28% of the total budget.

A further new feature is that ecological and socio-economic aspects will now be part of all programmes. Environment and quality of life run throughout the entire framework programme, and applicants would be well advised to take these aspects into account at the project concept stage.

The specific programmes in activity one focus on the following:

▸ **Information and communication technologies,** which were already prominent in the second and third framework programmes (ESPRIT, RACE, Telematics Systems), will be further developed.

Here work will concentrate on the creation of a *smart Europe*, since information and communication technologies are increasingly changing our economic and social environments, in such areas as working methods and relations, company organisation and training. This development leads to increased productivity, quality and efficiency in our economies. An *Information Society* is emerging in which the management and quality of information, together with the speed at which it can be transferred, have a marked effect on international competitiveness, and hence on growth and employment.

The Fourth Framework Programme sets out to build and expand new information structures: the development of computers into the *nerve centres* of an *infostructure* (information technology), access to and networking of these centres (communication technologies) and interaction with applications (telematics applications), such as traffic management, medicine and libraries.

▸ **Industrial and materials technologies** have been central to Community research funding for years. European industry, including small businesses, took a keen interest in the predecessor programmes (BRITE-EURAM, CRAFT) and played a successful part in them, as is borne out by the many successful patent applications resulting from the programme. A total of around ECU 2 billion is available for research in this area, including the **standards, measurements and testing** programme, and particular emphasis will be placed on the involvement of small businesses, which have enormous innovation potential in industrial technologies.

New materials, and the industrial technologies needed to develop and use them, are strategically important and indeed vital for Europe. Under the label *factory of the future,* work will concentrate on the development of smart design and production technologies. Work on new organisation models and better working conditions will also be promoted. Research into materials of the future, such as synthetic and ceramic materials, superconductors and composites, will be conducted in tandem with the development of related technologies, such as molecular engineering and nanotechnologies.

▶ The specific programme for **environment and climate** involves research into the natural environment and changes to the environment (global change), plus technologies for environmental monitoring, clean-up of environmental damage and risk management. The specific programme for **marine science and technology** is closely related, the aim being to understand unresearched phenomena of the sea as a total system. Both programmes take up subjects from the Rio and Berlin Conferences on the Environment. Given the high priority of research into global change, and the costs of coordinating this with the member states, it was only natural that the budget should be double that of the previous programmes at some ECU 1 billion.

▶ Environmental protection is also to the fore in the three specific programmes on energy research. The aim is optimal, safe use of various forms of energy. The **non-nuclear energy** programme has gained somewhat in significance with the inclusion of the hitherto independent THERMIE programme (demonstration projects on new energy technologies) in the framework programme. An important area is the research and use of alternative sources of energy, such as solar, wind and geothermal energy. A budget of ECU 1 billion is available for the whole programme.

▶ The two specific programmes on **nuclear fission safety** and **controlled thermonuclear fusion** guarantee the continuity of the extensive, internationally-recognised work carried out so far. The aim is to construct safe, environmentally-friendly reactor prototypes. Fusion research under the Fourth Framework Programme has two objectives: the construction of a new experimental reactor-together with Japan, Russia and the USA-known as ITER (international thermonuclear experimental reactor), and preparation of a demonstration reactor (DEMO) capable of generating significant quantities of electricity.

- The area of life sciences comprises the three specific programmes on biotechnology, where there is the expectation of enormous productivity increases, biomedicine and health and agriculture and fisheries. In genetic engineering, **biotechnology** provides one of the biggest growth areas in industrial countries. Applications cover a wide variety of areas from pharmaceuticals to food production, and since 1990 almost two-thirds of all new medicinal products have come from biotechnology. To keep pace with developments, work in the Fourth Framework Programme will concentrate on improving our basic biological knowledge of living systems (cell factory, genome sequencing, etc.).

- The **agriculture and fisheries** programme targets production improvements, the development of modern holdings and less-intensive, ecological agriculture and forestry.

- **Biomedicine and health** have long since been central themes of Community RTD policy. This is led by AIDS and cancer research, pharmaceutical research, and the new area of brain research.

**Finally, the specific programmes also tackle
two completely new research areas:**

1 *Transport* research (with 2% of the Fourth Framework Programme's financial resources) will help to develop large-scale traffic networks across the European Union, and to implement the common transport policy. Projects supported will include work on the integration of the various transport modes (air, sea, rail and road) into trans-European networks, along with traffic management systems, congested areas and environment and energy problems.

2 *Targeted socio-economic research* addresses research and technology policy options, and analyses the effects of research work on society in the sense of technology forecasting. There will be funding for work on general and vocational training – an increasingly important subject in view of the development of educational systems – as well as for work on the problem of social integration and exclusion (long-term unemployment, refugees) and finally technology assessment, a subject so far pursued in the USA and Japan, and also in Germany since the 1980s, but where little has been done at a European level.

Activity 2

| Cooperation with third countries and international organisations

Scientific and technical cooperation beyond European frontiers is essentially nothing new.

▶ The oldest framework for cooperation on European research began in 1971 with COST.

▶ 1985 saw the birth of the Franco-German initiative EUREKA which now has 25 members, including the European Commission.

In the Fourth Framework Programme for RTD, cooperation with European and non-European third (i.e. non-EU) countries have been brought together for the first time in a single programme. At the same time, the previous, limited subject divisions have been abandoned in favour of a geographical approach, which takes better account of the specific problems of different regions and economic zones.

The programme differentiates between three regions:
  ▶ **Europe, including Central and Eastern European countries, plus the New Independent States of the former Soviet Union**
  ▶ **non-European industrialised countries**
  ▶ **developing countries**

The programme has a budget of ECU 575 million to see it through to the end of 1998, the main funding being split equally between the Central and Eastern European countries and the New Independent States and CIS States, on the one hand, and developing countries on the other, with about 42% of the overall budget each. The rest is for cooperation with industrial third countries and international organisations.

Special rules apply for the participation of third countries in the research programmes and these are summarised in the following overview.

Participation of third countries in specific programmes of the Fourth Framework Programme for RTD

The following programmes are open:

Information technologies
Telematics applications
Advanced communication technologies
Industrial and materials technologies
Standards, measurement and testing
Environment and climate
Marine science and technology
Biotechnology
Biomedicine and health

Agriculture and fisheries
Non-nuclear energy
Nuclear fission safety
Transport
Targeted socio-economic research
Dissemination and
exploitation of results
Training and mobility
of researchers

Associated countries

Iceland - Israel - Norway - Switzerland *(agreement under negotiation)*
Liechtenstein

Participation under the same conditions as EU Member States

European third countries

Albania	Czech Republic	Malta	Slovenia
Armenia	Estonia	Moldova	Switzerland
Azerbaijan	Georgia	Poland	Turkey
Belarus	Hungary	Romania	Ukraine
Bulgaria	Latvia	Russia	
Cyprus	Lithuania	Slovakia	

Participation possible on a project basis.
Partners from these countries do not normally receive funding from the Community.
To facilitate participation for countries from Central and Eastern Europe and the States of the former Soviet Union and developing countries financial support is sometimes possible as part of the specific programme for International cooperation with third countries and international organizations.

Participation of third countries in specific programmes of the Fourth Framework Programme for RTD

Non-European third countries

Non-European third countries which have concluded an agreement with the EU on technical and scientific cooperation

Australia
  Biotechnology
  Biomedicine and health
  Marine science
  Environment
  Information technologies
  Communication technologies

Canada
  Agriculture and fisheries
  Biomedicine and health
  Non-nuclear energy
  Environment
  Information technologies
  Forestry research
  Communication technologies
  Telematics applications (economic and social development sector)
  Mineral processing

South Africa *(agreement initialled, May 1996)*

Participation possible as long as there is Community interest.
No Community funding of parties from these countries.

Non-European third countries which have not concluded an agreement with the EU on technical and scientific cooperation

Participation possible as long as there is Community interest and it is warranted through the principle of reciprocity. Participants from developing countries may receive limited funding as part of the specific programme for Cooperation with third countries and international organisations.

The following programmes are open:

Information technologies

Nuclear fission safety
(effects of radioactivity and historical liabilities)

Advanced communication technologies and services

Biotechnology
(pre-normative research, biodiversity, social acceptance)

Environment and climate

Biomedicine
(excluding pharmaceuticals research and biomedical technology)

Standards, measurements and testing

Targeted socio-economic research
(evaluation of RTD policy options)

Non-nuclear energy (R&D)

Marine science and technology

Transport

International organisations

Participation possible under the same conditions as European third countries. In certain cases international organisations with their headquarters in Europe can receive Community funding.

| Cooperation in Europe

COST - EUREKA - International organisations

Research in Europe has a long tradition and by the same token many facets. The framework programmes of the Community, while being a central component, are only part of a whole series of important international activities. The Fourth Framework Programme sets out to promote cooperation and interlinking with other European networks and international organisations. Priority is given to cooperation within COST, EUREKA, CERN, ESA, EMBL, ESO and ESF.

COST[1]

The 15 countries of the EU plus Switzerland, Norway, Iceland, Turkey, Czech Republic, Slovakia, Poland, Hungary, Croatia and Slovenia take part in COST actions. Cooperation may be in any area of research where there is sufficient interest amongst participating countries.

Two basic factors distinguish COST projects from Community research:
- planning is carried out jointly, but financing is on a national basis. Community funding is restricted to the services of the Secretariat and possibly financing of studies
- COST projects are not tied to predefined programmes, but instead operate *à la carte*.

In this way, over the years COST has introduced many new subjects into the specific research programmes of the Community.

At present there are more than 100 COST actions in 15 areas of research. Participation in a COST project is arranged via national coordination centres in the participant countries.

In the future, the European Commission plans to support COST cooperation beyond the current secretariat services, by evaluating and disseminating results and involving scientists from Central and Eastern European countries.

---

1 European COoperation in the field of Scientific and Technical research.
For information contact the COST secretariat run by the European Commission: Nicholas Newman, Rue de la Loi 200, B-1049 Brussels Tel: +32 2 295 59 76

EUREKA

Created in 1985 by 17 Western European countries and the European Community, EUREKA has grown vigorously in parallel to Community research. The number of projects has increased constantly and now totals more than 650 spread over 3,500 partners, including 2,400 from industry and small businesses. A total of ECU 14.5 billion has so far been invested in completed and ongoing EUREKA projects.

Community research programmes and EUREKA have very similar targets: a stronger technological base and better industrial competitiveness. From the outset the European Commission has championed this new form of European cooperation in research, and part-financed various projects. Despite the similarity of the research targets, the procedures are quite different, especially in terms of:

▸ *approach*: Whereas Community projects are mainly concerned with precompetitive and basic research, EUREKA projects are nearer to the market. Nevertheless, the demarcation lines are fluid and there are indeed EUREKA projects in basic research.

▸ *countries involved*: Since its creation, EUREKA has expanded geographically. In addition to the EU Member States and the European Commission there are now the former members of EFTA, Russia, Slovenia, Turkey, Hungary, Poland and the Czech Republic (25 in all).

▸ *organisation*: Whereas Community research is based on fixed institutional rules and pursues specific aims in its programmes, EUREKA projects arise more or less spontaneously without any overall planning (the *bottom-up* principle).

▸ *financing*: Decisions on funding and the extent of funding are taken by the national governments.

In the Fourth Framework Programme the clearly pre-competitive parts of EUREKA projects – provided they tie in with the aims of one of the specific programmes – can be funded with Community resources. In addition, the results of Community projects should be included and developed in EUREKA projects which are fundamentally nearer to the market. To this end, exchanges of information will be stepped up.

> *Anyone interested in becoming involved in EUREKA*
> *should contact the EUREKA Secretariat in Brussels*
> *or the national contact points for EUREKA.*[2]

---

2 **EUREKA Secretariat** - 19 H Avenue des Arts, Box No 3 - B-1040 Brussels
  Tel. +32 2 217 00 30 - Fax +32 2 218 79 06 - Telex 29340/EUREKA B

| International organisations

European scientific organisations do not only have enormous experience of their own, they can also draw on extensive networks, beyond the EU, of qualified scientists to supplement European cooperation in specific Community programmes. Cooperation with scientific organisations can thus be of great benefit for all project participants.

In the Fourth Framework Programme, such cooperation will be focused on the following international organisations:

- **CERN**   *(European Laboratory for Particle Physics)*
- **EMBL**   *(European Molecular Biology Laboratory)*
- **ESA**   *(European Space Agency)*
- **ESO**   *(European Southern Observatory)*
- **ESF**   *(European Science Foundation).*

Taking the cooperation agreements as a basis, the exchange of information will be improved, common interests identified and projects initiated.

| Cooperation with Central and Eastern European countries

The countries of Central and Eastern Europe[3] and the New Independent States of the former Soviet Union (NIS)[4] have considerable scientific and technological potential.

In Russia alone there were nearly three times as many scientists and engineers at the beginning of 1990 as in the European Community. In many areas, researchers from these countries are among the best in the world.

With recent upheavals in science and research, many of these researchers have lost their jobs. As a result, many highly qualified scientists are moving into other occupations or abroad, meaning that the scientific and technical potential essential to the rebuilding of these countries is being lost.

To counter this process, and to bring science and research in these countries closer to the European Union, in 1992 the Community began a ECU 55 million programme of RTD cooperation with Central and Eastern European Countries.

---

3   **CEE countries:** Poland, Hungary, Bulgaria, Romania, Czech Republic, Slovakia, Baltic states.

4   **NIS:** Armenia, Azerbaijan, Belarus, Georgia, Kazakhstan, Kyrgyzstan, Moldova, Russia, Tajikmenistan, Turkmenistan, Ukraine, Uzbekistan.

This was continued in 1993, and in 1994 through two main programmes which supported the participation in five specific programmes of the Third Framework Programme, and the creation of new joint projects and networks, respectively. These programmes are generally known as PECO-COPERNI-CUS and will continue within the new specific programme for *cooperation with third countries and international organisations*.

Support will be given to:

▸ individual initiatives in areas of particular interest to Central and Eastern European countries, or where they have special needs, e.g. research into clean energy, the environment and health

▸ INTAS (INTernational ASsociation for the promotion of cooperation with scientists from the New Independent States of the former Soviet Union) - research projects in which laboratories from the fifteen Member States plus Switzerland and Norway, on the one hand, and the NIS, on the other, can take part

▸ cooperative projects within specific programmes of the Fourth Framework Programme, all programmes being open to this.

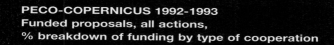

PECO-COPERNICUS 1992-1993
Funded proposals, all actions,
% breakdown of funding by type of cooperation

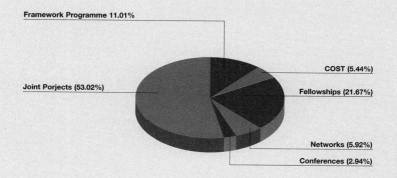

Framework Programme 11.01%

Joint Porjects (53.02%)

COST (5.44%)

Fellowships (21.67%)

Networks (5.92%)

Conferences (2.94%)

In addition to the activities under the Fourth Framework Programme, the European Union supports two further initiatives as part of scientific cooperation with Central and Eastern European countries and the NIS:

ACE - Action for Cooperation in Economics

ISTC - International Science and Technology Centre
Financial aid for RTD projects carried out by Russian scientists and institutions formerly engaged in military research.

Further information can be found in the brochure entitled
Scientific and Technical Cooperation with Eastern Europe,
published by the European Commission, DG XII.

This can be obtained from:
European Commission,
DG XII, Science, Research and Development
200 rue de la Loi
B-1049 Brussels
Fax: + 32.2.295.8220

| Cooperation with industrialised third countries

For these purposes, industrialised third countries are defined as:
- ► USA and Canada
- ► South Africa
- ► Israel
- ► Japan and Korea
- ► Australia and New Zealand

Contractual relations with these countries as well as rules for cooperation with parties from these countries can be seen in the overview of *Participation of third countries*, earlier in this section.

Cooperation in all areas of science, economics and the humanities is possible. In view of the economic and political implications, however, cooperation on projects with each of these countries will be restricted to specific subjects of common interest. Financing is through the respective programmes, which also show what individual subjects are open for cooperation with which industrialised third countries.

The Community will also continue to participate in the *Human Frontier Science Programme* initiated by Japan, through financing as part of the specific programme for *biotechnology*.

In addition, the number of grants for scientists and engineers wishing to carry out research in Japan will be increased to 50 per year. Support will be given to post-doctorate students, and young scientists who already have contact with Japanese research establishments.

In addition, a new programme will be started with Korea (5 grants per year).

| Cooperation with developing countries

The European Union has cooperated for some years now with the developing countries of Africa, the Caribbean and the Pacific in the fields of agriculture, industry and trade, health, energy and environmental protection on the basis of the Lomé Agreement. Scientific and technical cooperation has been supported by a number of initiatives as part of the RTD framework programmes and other specific measures.

▸ The **International Scientific Cooperation** programme has concentrated on Latin America, Asia and the Mediterranean. In 1993, a total of 160 research projects were funded and 165 grants were disbursed to scientists from those countries.

▸ The programme, **Science and Technology for Development**, part of the RTD framework programme since 1982, was geared to cooperation with Africa, Asia and Latin America in particular in life sciences. For 1991-94 a total of ECU 111 million was available.

▸ As part of the **AVICENNE** initiative for cooperation with Mediterranean countries not belonging to the EU, joint projects have been supported in the fields of waste water disposal, renewable sources of energy, and health.

In the Fourth Framework Programme these three initiatives are now all grouped together. The focus is on problems which are of fundamental significance for the future of the planet, such as the conservation of vital resources, contagious diseases, etc.

| Activity 3 |

| Dissemination and optimization of results

If research is to have a greater effect on the economy and on society than it has had in the past, action must be taken to facilitate easier and more efficient technology transfer.

The dissemination and utilisation of results will be particularly important in future to small businesses. The White Paper on *Growth, Competitiveness and Employment* highlighted Europe's weaknesses in failing to convert scientific results and technological achievements into industrial and commercial successes. Consequently, greater emphasis is placed in the Fourth Framework Programme on the development of operational mechanisms for technology transfer from research to industry.

An important feature will be measures to improve the business arena: scientific and technical information, financial services, protection of innovations, and training in new technologies.

Measures to disseminate and utilise results will be supported both within the specific programmes and as part of activity three.

The new specific programme, **Dissemination and optimization of results**, continues the activities of the third RTD framework programme (in particular the Innovation[5] Relay Centres and the CORDIS information system). In addition, activities will be introduced which have not so far been in the framework programme (in particular the former SPRINT programme and dissemination activities of the THERMIE programme, including the OPET network).

Technological change is seen more and more as a complex, dynamic process whose social and economic implications affect individuals, companies and institutions. Their ability to apply new knowledge through cumulative learning processes will depend heavily on the conditions being established for optimum development of innovations.

---

5 originally, Value Relay Centres

The new specific programme therefore targets three aspects of technology transfer and innovation:

- ▶ Creation of a business environment which facilitates the adoption of new technologies. Alongside European innovation monitoring and measures to improve the financial scenario, regional technology plans will be developed in conjunction with Directorate-General XVI (Regional Policy) which make it easier for small businesses in eligible regions to become involved in Community research.
- ▶ Dissemination of knowledge and technologies through networks. The plan is to expand the Innovation[6] Relay network as a universal, multi-programme consultation network and to promote sectoral transfer networks. The OPET network of energy technologies will be supported in the same way as selected technology transfer projects.
- ▶ Provision of technologies and services for the dissemination of information and knowledge. In this context the CORDIS information service will be further developed and information exchange between the Member States promoted.

Activity 4

| Training and Mobility of Researchers (TMR)

The training of young scientists at Community level has developed constantly in parallel to the university mobility programmes (ERASMUS, TEMPUS, COMETT, LINGUA). Young researchers have had the possibility for several years to study in recognised scientific institutions in other countries. The *Human Capital and Mobility* programme in the third framework programme considerably extended the range of these possibilities.

In the Fourth Framework Programme the training and mobility of researchers will be further intensified and a total of some 5,000 grants awarded. As a qualitative innovation, whereas in earlier programmes support was primarily for researchers with doctorates, the new programme is also open to scientists with research experience and in some subjects to doctoral students (after at least four years of study).

---

6 originally, Value Relay

The only change versus the Human Capital and Mobility programme in the third framework programme is that in the new programme there are only individual grants, the previous institute or group grants being dropped and replaced in part by the new concept of funding scientific networks (at least five partners from three countries). Support for access to major facilities remains, as does the possibility of financing Euroconferences and other accompanying measures.

Industrial laboratories will be included in the programme to a far greater degree than previously. Cohesion aspects will also be considered, i.e. the programme is open in particular to researchers from less developed regions of the Community who want to study in scientific establishments in the more developed regions. A list of disadvantaged regions is provided in the information package on the specific **Training and Mobility of Researchers** programme.

In addition to the activities of the TMR programme, training through research is also promoted in most of the specific programmes of Activity 1 (see "grants" within the specific programmes). While grants in this instance are awarded on a clear top-down basis, i.e. training measures must correspond with the respective targets of the programme, funding in the TMR programme is in accordance with the opposite bottom-up principle. Projects are permitted in the fields of exact and natural sciences, economic and social sciences and humanities provided they contribute to the aims of Community RTD policy and **cannot** be funded as part of other specific programmes of the Fourth Framework Programme for RTD.

An important technical innovation is a change in the status of TMR *fellows*. Since different taxation and social security systems imposed by national authorities on fellows have led to considerable discrepancies in net payments in the past, efforts will be made in future to ensure that TMR grants are more or less comparable with national or local salaries. Calculations will be based on net amounts plus national allowances (tax plus social and health insurance contributions, etc.).

4 | BEYOND THE FRAMEWORK PROGRAMME

Education and training to cope with industrial change

The Commission's White Paper on *Growth, competitiveness and employment* gives education and training a key role for the future development of the European Union. The innovative force of the European economy depends above all on the availability of adequately qualified experts for research and development and the conversion of research results into marketable products and processes.

Business and society therefore have a growing need for training and education, particularly in new technologies. The European internal market also needs qualified experts who are conversant with the conditions and opportunities in neighbouring countries, and who are motivated and able to work at a European level.

To this end, the Community - in addition to activities to promote young scientists within the RTD framework programme - has already done much in years gone by for the European dimension in general and vocational training. In less than 10 years, the Commission has introduced a wide variety of programmes to promote cross-border exchange between universities, companies and vocational training establishments, which in practice have been extremely well received, and have become a fixed component of the European training scenario.

These Community training programmes, aimed mainly at young people, permit them to do part of their studies abroad. There they can add to their qualifications, learn languages and gain valuable personal experience.

COMETT *(Community Action Programme in Education and Training for Technology)*, the programme to promote cooperation between universities and industry, was launched in 1986. Since that time 32,000 traineeships have been arranged in industrial companies and 6,000 training courses for company staff organised as part of university-industry training partnerships and courses in advanced technologies. Much new teaching material has also been developed.

ERASMUS *(European Action Scheme for the Mobility of University Students)*, a programme to promote mobility amongst university students, has been in existence since 1987. Almost 2,500 cooperative programmes between over 1200 university establishments, and a European Community Course Credit Transfer System (ECTS) in which 140 universities are currently participating, form the framework for the growing mobility of students in Europe. In the initial year, 1987, the Commission awarded about 3,500 grants, but by the 1994/95 academic year this had risen to some 127,000 grants to students from EU and EFTA countries, who can thus do a recognised part of their studies in another EU or EFTA country. Several thousand mobility grants have also been awarded to lecturers.

LINGUA *(Programme for the promotion of foreign language knowledge in Europe)* followed in 1990. It is geared to students and teachers of foreign languages. The results of the LINGUA programme are equally impressive: for the 1994/95 academic year some 10,300 exchange grants were awarded to students and a large number of teacher traineeships supported.

All three programmes drew to a close at the end of 1994. The evaluation which would determine whether or not to continue these training programmes proved highly positive. The programmes have achieved much both quantitatively and qualitatively, having promoted European awareness in universities and introduced European topics into curricula. This is clearly worth developing further.

At the same time, Articles 126 (Education) and 127 (Vocational training) of the Maastricht Treaty provide a new legal basis for extended cooperation in education and training, and thus scope for the inclusion of new factors in the funding programmes.

The most important feature of the new strategy is the focusing of previous activities along two main lines: the first covers all measures on general education (SOCRATES) while the second promotes vocational training (LEONARDO).

Both programmes came into being on 1 January 1995, with transitional arrangements being scheduled for 1995 in order to help channel the previous sub-programmes into the new structures of SOCRATES and LEONARDO.

The **SOCRATES** programme embraces two major predecessor programmes, ERASMUS and LINGUA, plus the smaller programmes of EURIDYCE (promotion of information exchange) and ARION (study visits for education specialists). A new feature is cooperation in the school sector. Total budget: ECU 850 million for 1995-1999.

In SOCRATES' Chapter I, which deals with cooperation between universities, the ERASMUS programme is continued as a sub-programme under the same name. Just over half the budget (55%) will be used for measures in this chapter, with the emphasis still on the mobility of students. The system of intra-Community recognition of partial studies (ECTS) will be geared up appreciably. Chapter II covers activities for pre-school, primary school and secondary school education, while Chapter III involves overlapping measures for all stages of education.

The **LEONARDO** programme sees the continuation of the previous programmes of PETRA (a programme for the vocational training of young people and their preparation for adult and working life), EUROTECNET (which promoted innovation in vocational training as a result of technological change), FORCE (development of continuing vocational training) and parts of LINGUA. The former COMETT programme will also be integrated. NB: Unlike the SOCRATES programme, none of the previous programme names have been kept.

The LEONARDO programme sets out to promote vocational training and to help improve vocational training systems in the Member States. Training and professional development are seen as equally important.

Most of the funds for LEONARDO will be used for trans-national pilot projects and exchange measures.

TEMPUS *(Trans-European Mobility Scheme for University Students)* is a programme geared primarily to the universities of Central and Eastern European countries which began in 1990 and was extended in April 1993 for a four-year period (TEMPUS II) beginning in the 1994/95 academic year. TEMPUS is part of the European Union's comprehensive programme for economic and social reform in the countries of Central and Eastern Europe (Phare) and of the programme to reform and assist the economy of the Republics of the former Soviet Union (Tacis).

To help eligible Central and Eastern European countries to develop and renew their university systems, grants are awarded to students, lecturers and administrative personnel. The Union also promotes measures to improve the education infrastructure and curricula. The basis is provided by cooperation programmes with university establishments from the EU Member States and the other G-24 countries.

Results to date: from 1990 to 1993 the EU supported a total of 639 TEMPUS projects. At present, teachers and students from some 1800 partner institutions are involved.

Research and development in the European regions

The structural differences within the Community (North/South divide) are far more marked in technological infrastructure than in purely economic terms (wealth/income). Article 130a of the Maastricht Treaty therefore advocates the strengthening of economic and social cohesion as one of the fundamental aims of the European Union, second only to completion of the internal market and establishing economic and monetary union.

The primary reasons for this regional divide in economic development are differences in productivity and competitiveness, which are in turn affected by the capacity to innovate and hence also by research and development.

To help offset these structural weaknesses, and as part of the allocation of the structural funds to the main targets of the common regional policy for the period of 1994-99, in 1994, research and development were included for the first time in the catalogue of measures of the structural funds.[7] This encourages companies, universities and research institutes to undertake RTD measures with a regional policy dimension.

---

7 European Regional Development Fund (ERDF), European Social Fund (ESF), European Agricultural Guidance and Guarantee Fund (EAGGF) - Guidance Section, Financial Instrument for Fisheries Guidance (FIFG) and Cohesion Fund.

Unlike the RTD framework programme, which only supports cooperation in research, the Structural Funds promote institutional measures, the most important being investments in infrastructure, which improve the underlying conditions for research and development, such as technology parks, trans-European networks in telecommunications, energy and transport, training and employment schemes plus equal opportunities for men and women at work.

To create synergistic effects between research and regional policy it was only natural to include the RTD framework programme as far as possible in the objectives of cohesion.[8]

This should not be taken to mean, however, that Community research funding is aimed at financial reallocation in favour of economically weaker Member States or regions. The main criterion is still the scientific quality of a project and the partners involved. In contrast to other financial instruments of the EU, research funding should be regarded more as a prize than a subsidy. This ties in with the basic rule that Community research funding is awarded without any regard to national quotas. Nevertheless, where projects are scientifically and technically equivalent preference may well be given to proposals involving participants from structurally weak regions.

Special efforts will be made to link RTD programmes and structural funds in favour of small businesses. In structurally weak regions in particular, the production industry consists primarily of small businesses which often do not have qualified staff, international partners, adequate services or financing conditions conducive to innovation.

---

8 Cohesion and RTD policy - synergies between research and technological development policy and economic and social cohesion policy - Commission communication to the Council and the European Parliament (COM(93)203 final) of 12 May 1993

Cohesion factors therefore play a special role in the Fourth Framework Programme, particularly in activities three (dissemination and utilisation of results) and four (training and mobility of researchers).

This involves the following:

Activity 3

Support for innovation and technology transfer services and infrastructure
▶ regional technology plans (RTP) - in conjunction with Directorate-General XVI -the aim being to make use of the possibilities under the structural funds and to encourage small businesses to take part in joint research programmes
▶ assistance for local and regional authorities and development organisations to build up regional innovation and technology transfer strategies and infrastructure (RITTS)

Activity 4

▶ Further training of scientists from structurally weak regions by means of periods spent at research institutes in better developed regions. An interesting innovation consists of return subsidies which allow fellows to continue their research work in their home countries.

PART 2

FROM THE IDEA
TO THE PROJECT

The following section concerns only the programmes of the Fourth Framework Programme (Part 4).

Different rules and procedures apply to the other programmes described in this guide. (Part 5).

1 | THE NEW STANDARD PARTICIPATION RULES

To ensure greater transparency and uniformity, on 21 November 1994 the EU adopted rules for participation in the Fourth Framework Programme.[1] These are based on Article 130j of the Maastricht Treaty.

Who can participate? (Article 1)

▶ Private and public companies
▶ Universities
▶ Private and public research institutes

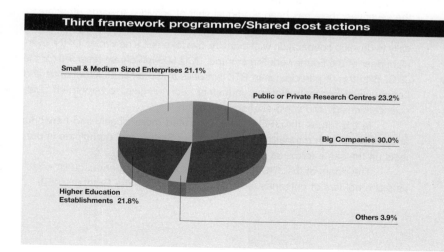

Third framework programme/Shared cost actions

Small & Medium Sized Enterprises 21.1%

Public or Private Research Centres 23.2%

Big Companies 30.0%

Higher Education Establishments 21.8%

Others 3.9%

1 Official Journal L 306, 30 November 1994.

▶ ... or, to put it in legal terms, every natural or legal person under public or private law who is resident or established in an EU Member State; the same applies to partners from third countries, which are participating in the specific programme concerned on the basis of an association agreement with the EU and are making a financial contribution to implementation of the programme. At the moment, this means Iceland, Israel, Liechtenstein and Norway, though negotiations are now also under way with Switzerland. Legally independent subsidiaries of undertakings from third countries with an association agreement can also participate, on condition that their research activities are conducted within the EU. Third (i.e. non-EU) countries with which a general framework agreement on scientific and technical cooperation has been concluded can also participate on a "project by project" basis.

The Joint Research Centre as partner

The Joint Research Centre (JRC), in which the EU's own research is carried out, can also participate in the specific programmes. The JRC consists of seven institutes, located in five Member States (Ispra/Italy, Geel/Belgium, Petten/Netherlands, Karlsruhe/Federal Republic of Germany and Seville/Spain). For many years, the emphasis was traditionally on nuclear research (Euratom). Since the seventies, there has been a gradual shift of activities towards other areas. With the Fourth Framework Programme, the JRC, which is seeking systematically to develop cooperation with industry, has taken on a new role.[2] Of the overall budget of the Framework Programme, ECU 600 million are reserved for the JRC. With this, it participates in RTD activities in the areas of information and communications technologies, industrial technologies, environment, biosciences, energy and socio-economic research.

In the future, the JRC will be integrated more closely into networks and consortia with partners from the Member States, and participate in projects on the same terms as industrial partners.

The doors of the JRC are also open to research groups, guest scientists and holders of bursaries (see "Joint Research Centre Grants", p152).

2 Conclusions of the Council of 26 April 1994 on the role of the Joint Research Centre (JRC), Official Journal C 126, 7 May 1994.

Information:
François Lafontaine
European Commission
DG XII - Joint Research Centre
Rue de la Loi 200
B-1049 Brussels
Tel: + 32 2 295 61 87
Fax: + 32 2 295 14 96

Important preconditions for participation (Article 2)

▸ Cross-border cooperation is one basic condition for support for research from the EU. You therefore need at least one partner from another EU Member State or a country associated with the Fourth Framework Programme (currently Norway, Iceland, Israel and Liechtenstein).

> *There is no general answer to the question of the optimum number of partners or the composition of the consortium. In a Community of 15 Member States with different technological potentials and requirements, it is clear, however, that the better balanced the combination and participation of the partners, the more attractive the project will be.*
>
> *In the final analysis, the objective requirements in each individual case are decisive. Of course, the success of a project does not depend primarily on the number of partners. Experience has shown, however, that individual projects involving more than four or five partners frequently require a disproportionate effort for coordination.*

▸ The partners must have adequate basic resources (technical, financial and management capacities) at their disposal. They should also be capable of utilizing the results of their work themselves, or of contributing to their dissemination and utilization.

International organizations and third countries as participants (Article 3)

International organizations, European third countries and non-European third countries, with which the EU has concluded a general framework agreement on scientific and technical cooperation (Australia and Canada; negotiations are under way with South Africa), can participate in projects in individual cases provided the specific programme decision allows such cooperation.

The precondition is a contribution of ECU 5 000 to the overhead costs of the project. Naturally, these participants cannot receive financial support at the expense of the EU.

Exceptions: In order to facilitate participation by countries from Central and Eastern Europe, the new independent states of the former Soviet Union and developing countries, financial assistance can be given within the framework of the specific programme for *Cooperation with third countries and international organizations*.

In certain cases, international organizations based in Europe can also obtain financial assistance from the EU.

When proposals can be submitted (Article 4)

The projects are selected on the basis of calls for proposals which are published in the Official Journal of the European Communities.

> **N.B.:** *In the interests of greater transparency, the Commission has decided on an important innovation: calls for proposals for all specific programmes will in future be published four times a year on fixed dates: 15 March, 15 June, 15 September and 15 December. In future, you can therefore prepare yourself for these dates in good time. You can obtain the text of the calls for proposals in all programmes from the Official Journal, or an overview from the issue of the RTD-Info newsletter published following those dates. Calls are also published electronically in CORDIS (RTD-news database and World Wide Web - http://www.cordis.lu).*

Expression of interest: Often the call for proposals is preceded by an invitation to express interest. In this way, potential participants obtain information in good time on areas of prime importance in the next call for proposals.

The call for proposals includes:

▶ description of the programme and its financial arrangements
▶ application procedure and deadlines
▶ financial contribution of the Community
▶ minimum requirements
▶ selection criteria

and also an address from which you can request a detailed information pack containing the work programme, forms for your proposal and other material.

In general you will have at least three months to submit your proposal. The Commission cannot give longer deadlines as, due to the large number of applications, the selection procedure is very time-consuming, and the programmes have to be completed within a fixed period of time.

Therefore, be sure to apply before the given deadline! If the time is too short for proper preparation of your proposal, it is perhaps better to wait for the next call. (It goes without saying that you should not wait for the publication of a call to begin putting your consortium together, and preparing your proposal.)

The Project Coordinator is responsible for ensuring that the proposal is submitted to the Commission within the stipulated deadline.

In some specific programmes, proposals on given subjects and activities may be submitted at any time. You will find more information on this in the relevant information packs.

What expenditure does a proposal involve?

According to Article 4.2 of the participation rules, the administrative costs which arise for the applicants in the preparation of proposals and for the Commission in the selection procedure are to be kept to a minimum.

For this reason, the application forms for all specific programmes have been standardized and streamlined considerably to keep the information to the minimum required.

Only when your project proposal has been accepted and the Commission invites you to enter into contract negotiations is further detailed information required. Of course, preparation of a proposal is both costly and time-consuming.

In particular, coordination between partners from various countries is often rather time-consuming; and, of course, it is advisable that you and your partners should agree on a common working language.

In the case of DG XII programmes, the proposal consists of two parts:
1. a form dealing with the administrative and financial aspects
2. a description of the scientific and technical content.

The administrative and financial form contains information on the participants, organization and costs, together with a brief description of the content (one page). This form is machine-readable, and you should therefore meticulously follow the instructions on how to fill it in. Experience has shown that a significant percentage (approximately 15%) of proposals are rejected because of failure to follow the formal procedures!

In the scientific and technical description of the project, the following information is requested:
- title;
- aims;
- anticipated results;
- state of the research;
- innovation potential;
- European added value;
- technical and economic added value;
- relationship to other EU research programmes and projects;
- contributions by the individual participants, project management, etc.

The extent of this description will vary from programme to programme. Fuller details are provided in the information packs on the individual programmes.

Basically, however, you should bear the following points in mind: Be as brief as possible, and as detailed as necessary. Above all, try to present your proposal in such a way that it is comprehensible. A concentrated, clearly set out and attractive presentation will considerably facilitate the selection task of the assessors, who have to cope with hundreds of such proposals, and this can in turn have a positive effect on the chances of your project. Brief and succinct statements accompanied, where appropriate, by charts and diagrams can increase your chances significantly.

Proposals relating to the programmes of DG III and XIII (information and communications technology) also contain a third, separate part with information on the consortium and the industrial aspects of the project.

In the information technologies programme, proposals on high-performance computer technology and systems and on long-term research are evaluated in two stages. In this way, unsuitable proposals can be filtered out at an early stage, and applicants are thus spared the expense of preparing a full proposal.

In principle, proposals can of course be submitted in any of the eleven languages of the European Union.

It is, however, advisable to submit a summary of the application in English if possible (in addition to the original in your mother tongue). This is not discrimination against other official languages but primarily in the interest of the applicants themselves as English has evolved –long before the EU came into existence and extending far beyond it– into the generally accepted "language of researchers" and it goes without saying that operations can be conducted more efficiently in this common language than in eleven different languages.

Pre-screening in the Brite-EuRam Programme

In the Industrial and Materials Technologies programme (Brite-EuRam), the Commission offers *pre-screening*, whereby applicants who have already prepared advanced project plans can receive guidance and recommendations for a complete application.

Proposals for pre-screening can be submitted by the project coordinator via the ARCADE information system (page 83) or to the following address:

Brite-EuRam
European Commission - DG XII
Rue de la Loi 200
B-1049 Brussels
Fax: +32 2 295 80 46

General selection criteria
for EC projects (Article 4.3)

Project proposals must in the first instance take into account the general criteria of the Framework Programme and also the special criteria of the relevant specific programme. You can see in detail what is involved in the information packs which you obtain from the Commission or via the Innovation Relay Centres.

In addition to the specific criteria for the programme in question, you should observe the following general selection criteria:

▸ Compliance with the subject and *aims of the programme*: this may appear self-evident, but is by no means always put into practice. The Commission is constantly striving for clearer formulation of the aims of the research, and it is up to the applicant to prove that the project corresponds to them.

▸ *Scientific and technical quality, innovative nature*
  • the project must correspond at least to the current state of the art
  • no duplication of results already obtained or of work currently being carried out on the same topic
  • if new technologies are to be tried out, describe why your proposal promises to be successful

▸ *European added value*: the principle of subsidiarity enshrined in the Maastricht Treaty (only projects which cannot be conducted better, more economically and more efficiently at another level - whether national or regional - are to be conducted at the Community level) requires substantial explanations regarding the effective European added value of a project. Sound reasons for deciding to submit the application at a European level will therefore be all the more important in future.

▸ *Cross-border cooperation*: at least two partners from different Member States; in the interests of balance, the inclusion of several partners from several Member States and, preferably, of different sizes is advisable.

▸ *Project management*: evidence of the partners' capacity to carry out cross-border projects, including the appropriate language abilities. Experience of management of European projects, particularly among the coordinators, may increase the consortium's chances.

▶ *Utilization and dissemination of results*: a criterion to which greater significance will be attached in future, even from as early as the project conception stage, as still greater emphasis will have to be placed on the targeting and success of EU research.

▶ *Social, economic and environmental effects* will play a major role in the Fourth Framework Programme as new, generally-applicable factors. Applicants are advised to consider these highly topical aspects as early as possible in the conception and formulation of their project.

In addition, the fundamental aims of EU policy should also be borne in mind, above all:

▶ completion of the *single internal market* which includes numerous research aspects, e.g. in the area of standards

▶ *cohesion* within the Community (bridging the gap between North and South within the EU, which is far wider in the case of technological infrastructure than it is on economic matters)

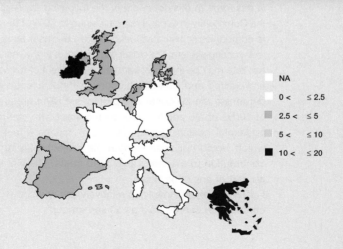

Total EC funding of Shared Cost Actions (2nd and 3rd Framework Programmes) as a percentage of total Government Appropriations

NA

0 <   ≤ 2.5

2.5 <   ≤ 5

5 <   ≤ 10

10 <   ≤ 20

Contracts with the European Commission (Article 6)

Once the projects have been selected, the Commission concludes a contract with the participants covering the administrative, financial and technical monitoring arrangements for the project, including intellectual property rights.

The financial contribution of the Community (Article 7)

In principle, the Community reimburses a large proportion of the project costs (generally up to a maximum of 50%); in return, this implies that the participants must provide a significant part of the funds themselves. The Community contribution depends on the aims of the programme and is announced in detail in the calls for proposals for the specific programmes.

In principle, support is available in the following forms:
- cost-sharing
- coordination of research activities
- fixed composite rates or fixed amounts

> *In the Fourth Framework Programme, cost-sharing continues to be the predominant and most valuable form of support. More than 80% of the funds available under the Framework Programme fall into this category, and all large-scale programmes are carried out in this form. In this connection, the following applies:*
>
> ▸ the Community in general reimburses up to 50% of the project costs to companies or institutes that operate a business management project-costing system; the closer the project is to the market, the lower this rate may be (contract with reimbursement of full costs)
>
> ▸ universities and other institutions without a costing system to determine the full costs of a project are reimbursed on the basis of 100% of the additional costs (contract with reimbursement of additional costs). "Additional costs" means direct expenditure which would not arise without the project, plus an appropriate contribution to the direct overhead costs. The Community pays no part of any other costs.
>
> For small projects involving relatively low costs, the Community's contribution can be paid as a fixed amount.

Important: The share of the project costs reimbursed is always limited to the maximum amount stipulated when the contract was concluded. No subsequent increases in the Community's share can be considered, even in the event of an unforeseeable overrun of the estimate.

Coordination (concertation)

This form of aid is restricted to RTD projects already financed by national, governmental or private bodies. In contrast to the cost-sharing system, the Community does not contribute to the costs of the research itself but just reimburses the administrative and networking costs (e.g. meetings, travel expenses) on the basis of flat rates. However, in this case it can reimburse up to 100% of the costs incurred.

As this form of support puts much less strain on the EU budget than cost-sharing, more areas can be covered and more partners can be involved.

This form of support will be extremely prominent in the Fourth Framework Programme, e.g. in the area of biosciences and biotechnologies, where there are a great many research activities spread over a broad spectrum.

Preparatory, accompanying and supporting measures

In this case, the Community contributes fixed amounts of up to 100% of the costs, e.g. to studies for supporting and assessing programmes or for drawing up future measures; it also supports training measures, scientific publications and activities for disseminating and utilizing the research results.

In addition, special measures, in particular on standardization, receive support of up to 100% of the costs in some programmes.

Special support for small businesses (Article 8)

The EU attaches particular value to broad participation by small businesses in the support programmes. The White Paper on *Growth, competitiveness and employment* highlights what influence small businesses have on growth and employment in the European Union. Above all, the potential of small, high-technology, industrial undertakings is of enormous importance for creating new jobs. It will not be possible fully to exploit the potential of the single internal market or to reduce structural unemployment without the driving force of small businesses.

According to the traditional definition of small business (fewer than 500 employees, annual turnover of less than ECU 38 million, not more than 33% of the capital owned by an undertaking which is not a small business), these undertakings account for more than two thirds of the jobs and turnover in the European Union. It is interesting that a corresponding proportion of all product innovations originate from small businesses. Far more creative and flexible than large organizations, they can react extremely quickly to new developments and market conditions. Their innovation potential means that they create many times more new jobs than all other participants in business life.

It is therefore important to attract small businesses to the research and technology programmes and to involve them in a more appropriate manner than previously.

The widespread preconception that EU research funding is aimed exclusively at large-scale industry and is suitable primarily for very large projects is therefore unrealistic and unhelpful.

At the same time it must be remembered that only a very small proportion of small businesses have their own research capabilities and that relatively few are involved indirectly in research work - for instance through membership of research institutes or contracts with research institutes.

As most small businesses are interested primarily in results and possible applications anyway, the high expenditure of carrying out their **own** research would barely be worthwhile.

In accordance with Article 130F of the Maastricht Treaty, the Community is responsible for assisting small businesses in their research and technological development efforts. Most specific programmes under the Fourth Framework Programme offer a great many starting points which are of special interest to small businesses also.

In some programmes, projects involving small businesses are even given preference if the proposals are otherwise scientifically and technically equal. In this connection, cooperation between small businesses and large enterprises can be highly advantageous, although it is in no way a basic precondition.

As the diagram on page 68 shows, the participation by small businesses in the Third RTD Framework Programme has concentrated on five specific programmes: information technologies, industrial and materials technologies, telematics, non-nuclear energies and communications technologies. 90% of the total small business involvement (or in absolute numbers 2174 participants) fell within these five programmes. If the 1200 participants in the CRAFT pilot action are added, almost half the small business participation falls within the industrial and materials technologies programme alone.

These thoroughly positive participation rates cannot, however, conceal the fact that between 1987 and 1993 an average, across all programmes, of only 19.8%[3] of the Community funds available for research and technological development went to small businesses.

---

3 The European Report on Science and Technology Indicators. Published by the European Commission. Luxembourg 1994, page 232.

The previously very unsatisfactory financial participation by small businesses in the Community's RTD programmes is structural and connected with the fact that it is difficult for these businesses to meet the frequently complicated administrative, legal, financial and management requirements.

With a view to making access to Community programmes easier for small businesses, special measures have therefore been included in 12 of the specific programmes under the Fourth RTD Framework Programme:

▸ in order to prepare well-founded proposals, awards can be granted for an exploratory phase, which also includes looking for partners

▸ small businesses with no, or only inadequate, research capabilities of their own can participate in joint research ("cooperative research") projects and in this connection have research work carried out for them by third parties. The CRAFT (Cooperative Research Action for Technology) joint research model, previously limited to Brite-EuRam, which has been developed on the basis of the AID (German Association of Industrial Research Institutes) support models, and has already proved its worth in the Third RTD Framework Programme, is thus being extended to all other programmes of interest to small businesses.

Approximately ECU 700 million are available for this new support for small businesses. The specific programme for *Industrial and Materials Technologies* is also of particular interest for the future. Up to 1998, a total of ECU 225 million has been reserved especially for small businesses in this area alone. Special attention will also be given to utilization of research results by small businesses.

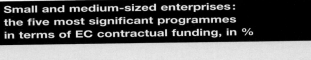

Small and medium-sized enterprises:
the five most significant programmes
in terms of EC contractual funding, in %

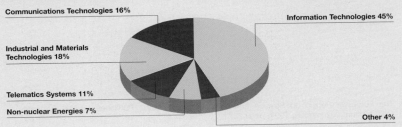

Communications Technologies 16%

Information Technologies 45%

Industrial and Materials
Technologies 18%

Telematics Systems 11%

Non-nuclear Energies 7%

Other 4%

Important features of the new approach to support for small businesses:

▸ For most specific programmes, the support will follow a uniform scheme. For 10 programmes, the framework conditions and advice on making applications are combined in a single three-part information pack.

▸ Proposals, both for exploratory awards and for joint research projects, can in general be submitted at any time. Selection takes place two or three times a year.

▸ The two-stage application procedure considerably reduces expenditure on project proposals. Only promising projects are recommended and supported to prepare a definitive proposal.

What will be granted:

Stage 1: Exploratory awards

Participation of at least two small businesses from different EU Member States or from one EU Member State and one associated third country

▸ to small businesses[4] with limited or no research capabilities of their own, in order to prepare a joint research project (allocation of research work to third parties: e.g. research institutes, universities or other undertakings)

▸ to small businesses with adequate research capabilities, in order to prepare a research project together with big businesses and/or research institutes. The final project proposal must then be submitted within the framework of the usual calls.

---

4 Small businesses are:
- businesses with fewer than 500 employees
- businesses with an annual turnover of less than ECU 38 million (in the information technologies programme ECU 50 million)
- businesses in which a maximum of 33% of the capital is owned by an undertaking which is not a small business.

Exploratory awards are available for expanding a project idea (e.g. working out a detailed work plan, looking for partners), including feasibility studies. Up to 75% of the costs, to a maximum of ECU 45 000, are reimbursed. The exploratory phase can last for up to 12 months.

> *N.B.:* Exploratory awards are not a precondition for participation in a stage 2 project. Proposals for joint research projects can, of course, also be submitted directly.

| Stage 2: Grants for joint research projects (cooperative research)

Participation of at least four small businesses from different EU Member States or from one EU Member State and one associated third country. Other industrial partners are allowed on a limited scale.

▶ In joint research, groups of small businesses without adequate research capabilities cooperate with institutes which carry out the research assignments.

Projects must correspond to the scope and objectives of the specific programme concerned; they should run for a maximum of 2 years and cost between ECU 0.3 million and ECU 1 million.

Subject to these conditions, the European Commission bears up to 50% of the total costs. Once again, the remaining 50% must be raised by the partners themselves (at least a third of the total costs must be borne by the small businesses).

Support for small businesses in the Fourth RTD Framework Programme 1994-1998

Specific Programmes	Exploratory awards	Cooperative Research
Combined in one info-pack		
Industrial and materials technologies	●	●
Standards, measurements and testing	●	●
Environment and climate	●	●
Marine science and technology	●	●
Biotechnology	●	
Biomedicine and health	●	●
Agriculture and fisheries	●	●
Non-nuclear energies (RTD projects)	●	●
Transport	●	●
Separate info-packs		
Information technologies	●	●
Communications technologies[5]		
Non-nuclear energies (demonstration)	special support scheme	

The application and selection procedure is simple and specially geared to the needs of small businesses.

If you are interested in this support for small businesses, you can apply to the contact persons for the individual programmes (see Part 4) or to the following address:

European Commission
DG XII - SME Coordination Unit
Mr Giorgio Clarotti
Rue de la Loi 200
B-1049 Brussels
Tel. +32 2 296 58 94 - Fax: +32 2 295 71 10

Also of interest are the supporting measures for small businesses in the specific programme for *Dissemination and optimization of results*.

5 provided in case small business participation is insufficient on first call

2 | PREPARATION OF A PROPOSAL

What is a typical Community project?

As a project proposal presupposes intensive preliminary work but, for financial reasons, not every applicant can be successful, it is strongly recommended that you check carefully whether the content and objectives of the project qualify for Community support and whether you are in a position to carry out or participate in a project of the size supported at Community level.

Whoever sets out on the Brussels road should above all be clear about the fact that the financial framework for Community support for RTD - measured against the RTD expenditure of many Member States - continues to be relatively modest while the number of scientifically impeccable applications is growing constantly. You should therefore first look around for other sources of financing at national level as well; this is particularly advisable if a project does not satisfy the selection criteria or include an adequate number of partners from other countries.

The question of the optimum number of partners and their origin clearly depends in the first place on the subjects, financial framework and aims of the specific programmes. As a result, in the past the average size of the consortia in the individual programmes varied widely, from 2.3 partners in the *Measurement and testing* programme to 14 partners in the case of aviation research.

Larger consortia are particularly common in the field of information and communications technologies where the average Community financial support is also relatively high (communications technologies: 9.5 partners/ECU 4.3 million; information technologies: 6.3 partners/ECU 2.6 million). In contrast, a typical project in the environment programme involved just five partners with total support of ECU 0.6 million.

On average across all programmes, five partners from three different countries took part in each project of the Third Framework Programme, and the average Community support was ECU 1.164 million.

Nevertheless, the idea that only large projects are considered for Community support is unrealistic.

Some programmes also lay down a financial framework for projects. In the new *Industrial and materials technologies* programme, for instance, the overall costs of a pure research project must lie between ECU 0.5 and 1.5 million. Industrial research projects, on the other hand, may be planned for between ECU 1 million and ECU 7 million. In each case a maximum of half the financial aid may go to any one individual partner or industrial group.

In the *biotechnology* programme, the large integrated projects must have 15 to 50 partners, with each partner receiving an average of approximately ECU 100 000 per year from Community funds, taking the total scale of such a large project to between ECU 1.5 and 5 million per year. For a *normal* RTD project with between 2 and 15 partners, the biotechnology budget envisages approximately ECU 0.2 - 1.5 million per project per year. Concerted actions (15 - 50 partners) should cost no more than an average of ECU 10,000 per partner per year, and studies can be funded up to a maximum of ECU 50,000.

One further example: for research networks in the specific programme for *Training and mobility of researchers*, a guide value of an average of ECU 50,000 to ECU 80,000 per partner per year is estimated, though the network coordinators can reckon on a higher allocation of funds for their expenditure. In order to put a limit on the number of partners, out of consideration for the workability of a network, the financial contribution to a single network for the total period of support of 3-4 years is to amount to ECU 1-2 million.

Sources of information and advice

Many potential applicants for Community research funding - in particular from small businesses - find it difficult to obtain information on the large number of EC support programmes, calls for proposals, the application procedures and the prospects of success.

At Community level, responsibility for initiating the flow of information from the Community to would-be-applicants rests with the applicants, and not with the Community authorities. Material of all kinds – newsletters, brochures and information packs on the specific programmes – is published in good time for each call under the Fourth Framework Programme and provides comprehensive, comprehensible and up-to-date information. At the same time the information system has been considerably tightened up, centralized and expanded, so that in future it will be possible to reach even broader circles. Nevertheless the geographical size and broad spectrum of industries interested in the Community programmes make it exceedingly difficult to keep track of all potential candidates in the Union and to provide them with a continuous flow of information from Brussels.

It is therefore extremely important that everyone interested should take the initiative of making themselves known, and of securing the relevant information. In practice, this means that while the Commission will supply information packs, brochures, etc. by return and free of charge, it will naturally do so only on request. In order to speed up the flow of information, it is advisable to write directly to the contact persons for the specific programmes *(see address list in Part 4)*.

A recent innovation in this area is the opening of a site for DG XII on the World Wide Web. There, interested parties can keep themselves informed of the latest developments, request brochures and other information, and even download work programmes and information packs via the CORDIS electronic document delivery service.

DG XII's home page URL is
http://europa.eu.int/en/comm/dg12/dg12tst2.html
and the CORDIS URL is **http://www.cordis.lu**

Some programmes publish regular periodicals to keep interested parties up to date with useful information. It is also possible to be put on the mailing list of a specific programme.

One special feature of Community research funding is that the Commission staff involved are directly accessible to interested parties. In contrast to other EU funds, no national administrative body is involved. As a result, and particularly in the initial stages, the high ratio of potential applicants to Commission staff can make communications difficult. Nevertheless, the ability to submit an application directly to the decision-making body should be seen as an opportunity rather than a problem.

To help mitigate any communications problems, the preparation and handling of Community research projects can be carried out with the aid of advice centres.

Through these, you can first clarify whether your project is actually eligible for Community research funding and which programme you should consider, and find out about application forms and deadlines, selection criteria, partner questions and financing conditions. This can save you a great deal of time, money and, perhaps, disappointment. **Above all, therefore, make sure that you obtain adequate information in good time.**

You can obtain information from the following agencies:

CONTACT CENTRES

▶ Contact centres in the Member States

For all specific RTD programmes, there are highly competent contact persons in the individual EU Member States with many years of experience who often also specialize in individual programmes. They provide information on calls for proposals, application procedures, prospects of success, etc.

The national contact persons are in constant touch with the Commission officials responsible for the programmes and are also informed about all the latest developments.

▶ **European Commission**

If the contact persons in the Member States can offer no further help, you should turn to the contact persons for the individual programmes at the Commission who are listed in Part 4. In general, they will also find contact persons to whom you can speak in your mother tongue. Potential applicants keen to contact the Commission officials responsible are always met with great openness and accessibility. However, for legal and practical reasons, the Commission cannot, for instance, systematically advise partners.

▶ **Briefing sessions**

The European Commission frequently organizes briefing sessions in the Member States or in Brussels, in particular for the programmes relevant to industry, usually on the occasion of the publication of the call for proposals. They afford an opportunity to obtain information at first hand, to discuss projects with representatives of the Commission and, possibly, to find potential partners for joint research projects.

▶ **Innovation Relay Centres**

In order to assist in the utilization of the results of Community research, since the beginning of 1993 the Commission has set up a new network of RTD liaison offices known as *Innovation Relay Centres*[6] in the Member States. Although their primary task is to promote technology transfer, these centres provide information on all details of Community research and technology programmes and calls for proposals. They are intended in particular to facilitate access to EC research and its results for small businesses, for instance by identifying suitable programmes, providing contact persons, seeking and providing cooperation partners or settling financial and contractual questions.

   The network of Innovation Relay Centres is being systematically extended within the framework of the specific programme for *Dissemination and optimization of results*.

6   originally, Value Relay Centres

▸ **Euro Info Centres**

The Euro Info Centres (EIC), which have been set up by the European Commission in all Member States, provide information on RTD programmes and other sources of support, and all business-related activities of the European Union. The range of services is geared especially to the needs of small businesses. You can obtain further information and contacts from chambers of industry and commerce.

▸ **FEICRO - Federation of European Industrial**

Cooperative Research Organizations

This is a network specially for small businesses interested in joint research. Approximately 300 joint industrial research institutions from 15 EU and EFTA countries are affiliated to it. FEICRO supports research and development in small businesses at a European level through information, advice and assistance for participation in European research programmes.

> Further information:
> **c/o IRSIA - George Allo**
> 6, rue de Crayer
> B-1050 Brussels
> Tel. +32 2 643 25 27
> Fax: +32 2 643 24 32

▸ **EACRO - European Association of Contract Research Organizations**

Contract research organizations from various European countries have joined together to form EACRO. The network, which at present has approximately 50 members, can also help in identifying and bringing together potential partners.

> Further information:
> **EACRO**
> B.P. 3
> F-78373 Paris Cedex
> Tel. +33 1 34 81 85 81
> Fax: +33 1 30 54 04 14

▶ BC-Net - Business Cooperation Network

BC-Net is an computer-based network to which at present some 600 business consultants are connected. The aim is to provide partners at a European level in all areas of business cooperation.

Contact: **European Commission, DG XXIII,**
Tel. +32 2 296 23 46
+32 2 296 28 08.

Other contact centres

Information on Community research funding is also available at a national and regional level in the Member States from associations (trade associations, chambers of industry and commerce) and business liaison organizations.

Many business consultants have also discovered the EU as a market. Take care which one you choose, and do not allow yourself to be talked into believing that in Europe financing is available for **everything**.

WRITTEN INFORMATION

▸ **Official Journal of the European Communities**
The most important official source of information is the Official Journal of the European Communities, in which Commission proposals, Council decisions and calls for proposals for individual programmes are published. More specifically, it contains:

- official notice of Commission proposals on new research programmes and calls for proposals **(in the C series)**
- Council decisions on research programmes **(in the L series)**
- Commission calls for proposals and expressions of interest **(in the S series - Supplement).**

> Available from:
> **Office for Official Publications of the European Communities,**
> 2, rue Mercier
> L-2985 Luxembourg,
> tel. +352 49 82 81.

However, if you are interested in a particular programme, do not wait for official publication of a call for proposals in the Official Journal. Start gathering more detailed information about the content and aims without delay. In this way, you can give yourself a few extra months in which to prepare your proposal.

▸ **Information packs**
If you are planning to prepare a proposal, you will in any case need the information pack on the specific programme which is of interest to you. It contains everything you need to know for conception and formulation of a project proposal: detailed programme description, work programme, participation conditions, application forms, etc. Information packs can be obtained free of charge on request from the contact persons for the individual programmes at the European Commission, or directly from the World Wide Web (see above).

> **RTD INFO**

Launched in July 1993, this bi-monthly newsletter is published in German, English and French by the Commission's DG XII. It contains up-to-date information and reports on new developments in the Community research programmes (e.g. current calls for proposals, contact persons, dates of information events, scientific and technical publications).

Available free of charge from:
European Commission
DG XII - Information and Communication Unit
Rue de la Loi 200
B-1049 Brussels
Tel. +32 2 295 64 19
Fax: +32 2 295 82 20

> **Innovation and Technology Transfer**

Published in English, French and German, this newsletter focuses, as its name suggests, on all EC activities relevant to innovation and technology transfer, including general policy, news from the Innovation programme, results and activities of the specific programmes, case studies, upcoming conferences, and new publications.

Available free of charge from:
European Commission - DG XIII - D 2,
JMO B4 - 082
L-2920 Luxembourg
Fax: +352 4301 32084

COMMUNITY DATABASES
AND INFORMATION SERVICES

▶ CORDIS

The Community Research and Development Information Service (*CORDIS*) consists of a set of on-line databases offering information covering programmes, projects, partners, etc. In addition, there is a database of RTD news, updated daily, and available in three languages (*English, German, French*).

Important innovation: in September 1994, a CORDIS World Wide Web (WWW) server was also introduced (accessible only via Internet, **URL: http://www.cordis.lu/**). Through this, you can obtain the full text of documents such as work programmes and information packs on the specific programmes. You can also reach CORDIS via the bulletin boards (BBS) run on the same server. CORDIS is accessible via ECHO (*European Commission Host Organization*).

Find out how to become an ECHO user from:
ECHO-CORDIS Customer Service
Post box 23 73
L-1023 Luxembourg
CORDIS Help desk
Tel. +352 34 98 12 40
Fax: +352 34 98 12 48
E-mail: helpdesk@cordis.lu

The contents of the CORDIS databases is also available on CD-ROM, which is available on a subscription basis. Subscribers receive an updated CD-ROM every three months.

For subscriptions, contact:
EUR-OP
OP4C - OFL
Tel: +352 2929 420 17
Fax: +352 2929 420 27

CORDIS Focus provides written information in the form of extracts from the RTD News database. *CORDIS Focus* appears fortnightly, and is also available in French and German.

Available free of charge from:
European Commission - DG XIII D/2
Dissemination of Scientific and Technical Knowledge
L-2920 Luxembourg
Tel. +352 43 01 331 61

▶ **World Wide Web**
Like many other parts of the Commission, DG XII now provides information via the multimedia part of the Internet, the World Wide Web (itself developed from its origins at CERN, under a Community research project.) The objective is to provide reliable and up-to-date information on RTD to all interested parties, while giving them a chance to respond through the *feedback* service. The information provided includes a directory of DG XII, contact points for the various programmes, news of all kinds, and many links to other relevant sites. It is even possible to request brochures and other information, and to consult or download work programmes and information packs by means of the link to the CORDIS electronic document delivery service. DG XII's home page URL is: http://europa.eu.int/en/comm/dg12/dg12tst2.html

► **ARCADE**

ARCADE (*Ampere Remote Control Access Data Entry*) is a data communication service developed by the European Commission - DG XII - which is used in particular for the programmes of DG XII. Operating in interactive mode, it offers various kinds of information, e.g. on making applications and on work programmes. ARCADE can also provide help in seeking partners by accepting expressions of interest.

ARCADE can be reached via public Videotex networks (Bildschirmtext, Télétel and Prestel standards),[7] via X.25,[8] dial-up telephone,[9] and Internet.[10]

Information:
European Commission
DG XII/ARCADE Office
Rue de la Loi 200
B-1049 Brussels
Tel. +32 2 295 07 45
Fax: +32 2 296 06 26

► **RTD Help-Desk**

From this information service, you can obtain, by telephone or in writing, information on research activities of Community contact persons and information sources for individual programmes.

Contact:
RTD Help-Desk - Dissemination of Scientific and
Technical Knowledge Unit - DG XIII D/2
European Commission
L-2920 Luxembourg
Tel. +352 4301 331 61
Fax: +352 4301 320 84

---

7 Belgium, Denmark, Greece, Ireland, Netherlands - **access code Arcade**
   Germany, Spain, UK, Portugal - **access code *Arcade#**
   France, Luxembourg - **access code Eurarcade**
   Italy - **access code *3615021#**
8 NUA (+206) 228840300
9 +322.2963702 (baudrate 1200/75), +322.2963707 (1200), +322.3963712 (2400)
10 telnet.arcade.cec.be (from a telnet session)

The role of coordinator, contractors and associated contractors

Community projects are in general conducted by consortia with participants from several EU Member States. It is advisable to clarify from as early as the application stage which role the individual participants are to play. The different roles bring with them different rights and obligations.

▸ **Contractors**
Contractors participate in the financing and performance of the project.

A distinction should be drawn between:
- *contractors*, who sign the contract with the Commission and are, within reasonable limits, jointly and severally liable for the performance of the contractually stipulated work. They are accordingly fully entitled to exploit the results of the project.
  The contractors can draw up a consortium agreement among themselves which, inter alia, stipulates the details concerning utilization and exploitation of the results of the project. These arrangements must not, however, conflict with the provisions of the Community standard contract.

- *associated contractors*, who participate technically and financially in a project but are not involved in signing the contract with the Commission and are not liable. Accordingly, their rights to exploit the results - and, in particular, their right of access to the results of other programmes - are limited. The contractors must, however, grant them such rights to an appropriate extent. The associated contractors agree with the contractors an association contract which as a rule must be approved by the Commission. In this connection, the principles of the standard contract are to be observed.

▶ The project coordinator

The project coordinator must come from among the contractors. He is the connecting link between the participants and the Commission and should therefore possess appropriate project-management experience and the necessary level of technical competence. The coordinator is responsible for performance of the entire contract. His tasks include:

- submission of all documents and technical reports on the progress of the project within the given deadlines
- passing on payments from the Commission to the other partners in the project (where no direct payments from the Commission to the partners have been agreed)
- clarification of all practical and legal matters which may arise during the period covered by the contract (the determining factor usually being the law of the country of origin of the coordinator)

▶ Subcontractors

Subcontractors conclude a contract with one of the contractors or associated contractors. No direct rights and obligations are imposed by the contract with the Commission. They work directly for one or more contractor(s) and are paid for the full cost of their work. Subcontracts are in general not the concern of the Commission, but they must be approved by the Commission if the subcontractor comes from a third country or an associated state, or if his services account for more than 20% of the contractor's total costs.

Planning for project costs

In RTD projects, the financial contribution of the Community is generally up to 50% of the eligible costs. This applies both for contracts with full-cost reimbursement and for contracts with reimbursement of marginal costs.

The following costs are reimbursed under the new model contract for the Fourth RTD Framework Programme.

Direct costs:

▸ *Personnel:* Scientific personnel, technical support and experts/specialists who work directly for the project. In the case of full-cost contracts, either the actual current costs or average salaries (provided they do not differ considerably from the actual costs) can be used as a basis.

In the case of marginal cost contracts (universities), the actual current costs are used. The following can be financed:
- additional temporary personnel who are employed directly for the project
- the cumulative working time of personnel who are already employed in the framework of other external resources (part time).

The working time spent on the project is to be documented.

▸ *Durable equipment:* Bought or leased equipment to the extent that it is required for the project. Computers with acquisition costs of up to ECU 25 000 can be written off at 33% per year, i.e. in three years; for other equipment, the writing-off period is five years or 20% per year.

> *N.B.: in the case of projects shorter than the writing-off period, a corresponding proportion of the acquisition costs is borne in full by the participant.*

▶ **Third party assistance:** Costs for subcontracts and other third party services.

▶ **Travel:** Travel and subsistence expenses for travel inside and outside Europe. For travel outside Europe, approval from the Commission is necessary.

▶ **Consumables and computer costs:** Can be reimbursed as direct costs. In the case of full-cost contracts, these costs are to be placed under overheads as indirect costs as far as is practicable.

▶ **Specific project costs:** Additional and unforeseen expenditure (including equipment prototypes) - only after written approval by the Commission.

Indirect costs - overheads

▶ General administration and secretarial costs, management, buildings costs, depreciation of buildings and general equipment, office equipment, maintenance, post, telephone, heating, electricity, medical service, on-the-job training and insurance.

For full-cost contracts (industrial firms), the proportion of indirect costs attributable to the project must be properly documented.

For marginal-cost contracts (universities), up to a maximum of 20% of the additional project costs can be charged as overheads without being documented.

Non-reimbursable are: profits, costs of sales, marketing and advertising, reserves against future losses or liabilities, interest calculated for costing, turnover taxes or customs duties.

Example	
Personnel	145 000
Computer	20 000
Travel	15 000
	180 000
plus 15% overheads	27 000
Third party assistance	15 000
Total	247 000

Considerable flexibility: In the Community research programmes, as a rule transfers are allowed between all types of costs, i.e. savings in personnel can be used for equipment and vice versa, provided the project is not significantly modified as a result. The possibility also exists of transferring costs from one partner to another provided the consortium is in agreement on this. There is also flexibility with regard to time within the period of the project, so that, for example, any additional expenditure incurred in the first year can be offset by savings made during the second year. In order to be entirely sure that such changes are accepted by all participants, however, you should obtain the approval of the Commission.

But be careful: if you exceed the overall cost planned, you must bear the extra costs in full.

The 10 golden rules for applicants

▸ **Selection criteria:** Pay close attention to the selection criteria given in the calls for proposals and the information packs! If your proposal does not fulfil all the criteria, give it time to mature, and wait until the following call for proposals.

▸ **Advice:** Take advice before you make your application. Find out in particular whether your project conforms with the general aims of the programme.

▸ **Financing:** Ensure that you can finance your share of the project. Normally this is 50 % of the costs; for universities (marginal cost contract), this can be in the form of deployment of existing personnel or resources.

▸ **Form:** Be sure to make the application on the appropriate form. This will speed up processing in the Commission and ensure your anonymity during the selection procedure!

▸ **Deadlines:** Invitations to submit project proposals are published at regular intervals and on the same dates four times a year (15 March, 15 June, 15 September and 15 December). Proposers often find the deadlines tight, but they must be met.

▸ **Closing date:** The closing date is usually set for the middle of the week at midday. Proposals must be submitted by the indicated time. It is not the postmark but the date of receipt at the Commission which counts. In general, up to 10% of proposals are rejected because they arrive after the closing date.

▸ **Presentation:** The presentation of your proposals should be generally comprehensible, clear and attractive. Among the many applications, success usually goes to those that are directly convincing. This includes a summary of the proposal on a few pages which can give the assessors an initial overview and impression of the quality of the proposal.

▸ **Completeness:** Although the European Commission has automated the processing of applications, it has neither the time nor the personnel to request missing parts of proposals received, given their great number. Incomplete applications therefore have little chance.

▸ **Signatures:** Each proposal must of course be approved and signed by all partners in the project. Observe any special instructions on signing.

▸ **Copies:** For efficiency reasons, the Commission generally requests applicants to send five copies of their proposal which are then distributed to the assessors and the relevant Commission departments.

3 | PROJECT SELECTION AND CONTRACT NEGOTIATIONS

The procedures for selection of eligible projects and the subsequent contract negotiations occasionally lead to uncertainties and misunderstandings for participants and other parties interested in Community research funding.

The Commission has therefore published a handbook which gives an insight into the handling of project proposals and an introduction to the contract negotiations.[11]

There is a step-by-step explanation of what happens to project proposals received at the Commission, who is involved in the selection procedure, who decides, and what then happens with the proposals which are selected and those which are rejected.

How the decision is made

The decision on the proposals is taken in a multi-stage procedure:

Stage-1 **Receipt and registration of the proposal**
The proposals received are held in safekeeping until the deadline has passed and only then opened, registered, provided with a reference and checked for completeness.

Stage-2 **Screening**
Commission employees first screen all proposals and filter out those which fail to satisfy the minimum criteria.

---

11 EC-funded research and technological development- an insight into the handling of project proposals; an introduction to contract negotiation (Office for Official Publications of the European Communities, 1994, ISBN 92-826-7076-7)

`Stage-3` Selection of external experts

The scientific and technical assessment of the project proposals is carried out by independent experts from the Member States. As a large number of applications is usually received, many assessors are required in the interests of rapid completion of the selection procedure. The experts are proposed, inter alia, by the members of the programme committees and also by scientific and specialized institutions, but enterprises and institutes can also put names forward to the Commission. In some programmes, the Commission also publishes calls for proposals for the selection of experts. The assessors are contractually bound to absolute confidentiality. At each new selection round, at least a third of the experts are replaced.

`Stage-4` Assessment

In the first phase of assessment, an assessment system agreed with the relevant programme committee is used to check how far the selection criteria, which are explained in the information packs, are satisfied. At this stage, the assessors have no knowledge either of the identity of the applicant or of the country of origin of the proposal. Only when project management and financing plans are assessed, do they have access to information on the participants. After individual assessment of the proposals, an attempt is made, under the leadership of the Commission, to bring the assessors to a common point of view with regard to marking.

If considerable differences of opinion emerge at this point, a further assessment may be necessary.

`Stage-5` Establishment of an order of priority of the proposals

Based on the marks and statements of the assessors, a list of proposals is drawn up divided into four categories:

▸ **very good:** the proposal is recommended for support, with no or minor modifications
▸ **good:** the proposal is interesting but still requires some modifications
▸ **work needed:** the proposal can be considered only if adequate funds are available, possibly with considerable modifications
▸ **not retained:** the proposal is not acceptable.

The list is sent to the members of the relevant programme committee.

Stage·6 List of projects worthy of support

Before the programme committee meets, the Commission draws up a list of projects worthy of support. This takes into account the marks of the assessors, other political considerations of the EU and the funding available. Normally, the very-highly rated proposals are selected. Only if too many proposals qualify from a limited subject area may lower-rated proposals, from other subject areas, be given a chance in order to achieve the aims of the programme.

Stage·7 Statement of the programme committee - Final list

The relevant programme committee discusses the proposed list and gives its opinion. It is then agreed which projects are to be supported in any case, and which are to be put on a reserve list for possible support.

Stage·8 Final approval - decision procedure

The final decision on which projects are to receive support, and how much, rests with the Commission, which makes a decision in a formal legal procedure.

Stage·9 Notification of acceptance or rejection of the project

The project coordinators are informed in writing whether their project has been accepted, put on a reserve list for possible subsequent support, or rejected.

Contract negotiations made easier

If the application was successful, the project coordinators are invited to contract negotiations - in many cases to Brussels or Luxembourg. As a rule, the usual standard contract is concluded. In preparation for the contract negotiations, the applicants must provide more sophisticated information on the structure, implementation and costs of their project. For this they receive forms which must be completed within a specified time and submitted to the Commission.

> **N.B.:** it is essential that the deadlines set during the contract negotiations are observed. Otherwise the Commission has the right to break off the negotiations.

The sequence of the contract negotiations is described in detail in the brochure "EC-funded Research and Development - Part 2: An Introduction to Contract Negotiations".[12]

Please note that work on the project may not be started until every stage of the contract negotiations has been completed, and the contract has been signed by the partners and the Commission departments responsible. In general, the project starts on the first day of the month following signature by the Commission. Costs incurred before this date cannot be reimbursed by the Commission, nor can costs which arise during the contract negotiations, for example for travel to preliminary discussions.

12 ibid.

PART 3

WHAT COMMUNITY
RESEARCH CONTRACTS COVER

PART ③

1 | THE NEW SIMPLIFIED MODEL CONTRACT

The standard contract[1] developed by the Commission in 1988 has basically proved successful. However, with the Maastricht Treaty and the further simplification being requested by various project participants changes were needed.

The main changes concern:
- stronger project management;
- participation of partners from outside the EU (Council Decision of 21 November 1994 concerning rules for participation in the specific programmes pursuant to Article 130j of the EC Treaty[2]);
- clarification of relations with associated contract partners;
- participation of the Joint Research Centre in the specific programmes;
- possibility of direct Community payments to individual parties.

The new model contract also contains slight changes in the rules on intellectual property rights,[3] and the rules on the utilisation and dissemination of results have been aligned with the general rules for the dissemination of research results[4] adopted on the basis of Article 130j of the EC Treaty.

---

1 Model contracts for activities in the field of research and technological development.
  To be obtained from the contact persons for specific programmes given in Part 4.
2 OJ No L 306, 30.11.1994, p. 8.
3 Model contract for Community activities in the field of research and technological development
  (Fourth Framework Programme).
4 OJ No L 306, 30.11.1994, p. 5.

The contract consists of four elements

- The actual text of the contract covers only a few pages: essential conditions of the contract, contract partners, title and duration of the project, total costs and financial participation of the Commission, report deadlines and special conditions.
- **Annex I** describes the work programme: content and aims of the project, contributions by the individual participants.
- **Annex II** contains the *General Conditions for performance of the project*: tasks of the coordinator and project partners, participation of third parties, termination of contract, conditions governing the use of results and exchange of know-how and licences, reimbursable expenses and reimbursement procedures.
- **Annex III** contains special conditions for the respective specific programme.

Further annexes may, where necessary, lay down special conditions for the particular project.

The contract can be concluded

- as a contract with full cost-sharing (the Commission's contribution usually being limited to 50% of the total cost);
- as a contract with reimbursement of marginal costs (the Commission reimbursing 100% of actual marginal costs);
- or as a contract with a fixed contribution from the Commission.

The contract is approved and signed by all contractual partners, with the coordinator being responsible for project management. While the contract is usually subject to the law of the coordinator's country of origin, the European Court of Justice has sole jurisdiction in disputes between the Commission and the contractual partners.

2 | CONTRACT MANAGEMENT AND PAYMENT SCHEDULE

Even experienced participants in Community RTD funding are sometimes unclear as to financial accountability and technical reporting, but in the interest of correct contract management these procedures cannot be ignored and certain deadlines and payment rules must be observed.

The management of Community projects is in many ways much more flexible than is the case with other forms of financing. A major advantage, for example, is approval for the entire duration of a project. Funds are not tied to individual budget (i.e. calendar) years and can be adjusted to the project's progress. A further advantage is the transferability of different types of cost, i.e. shifts between personnel, operating and investment expenses are permitted as long as the overall budget is kept to.

> **NB.:** To speed up the payment processes, amongst other things, the new model contract provides for the possibility of direct Commission payments to individual contractual partners, i.e. without going via the coordinator. However, payments via the coordinator remain the rule.

The following rules are important for contract management:

| Start-up of project

A project cannot begin until the Commission has signed the contract. As a rule, projects will start on the first day of the month following signature. Costs arising before that date, including expenses in connection with contract negotiation, will not be refunded except for costs for long-term machinery and equipment purchased within a period of six months before the contractual start date.[5]

| Contact with the Commission

An official at the Commission is in charge of each project and the project coordinators can contact him at any time. Some programmes need external experts as technical assessors who consult the Commission officials, e.g. where a contract is to be changed. In many cases the technical assessor is the first contact point for the project coordinator.

| Contract changes

Changes in the contract and the Technical Annex must be agreed with the Commission. This applies in particular to any departure from the design, cost or work programme and any changes in the consortium. Where contractual partners cannot meet their obligations the Commission must be informed immediately.

| Payments

Payments for EC-funded research projects are always in ECU and are usually made to the project coordinator, who is responsible for forwarding payments to the other contract partners. To protect the consortium from any insolvency, it is recommended that a trust account be set up for the project. Under certain circumstances, however, direct payments from the Commission to individual contractual partners can be arranged.

---

5 The same applies in the new model contract to machinery and equipment bought as part of an earlier contract concluded with the Community where such machinery and equipment has not fully depreciated.

Advance payment

In the Fourth Framework Programme the Commission will continue its practice of advance payments, one which is relatively generous in comparison with other funding systems. This will help to avoid any long pre-financing periods for the contractual partners, and offset any delays in payments. For a typical three-year project with annual payments, for example, the coordinator usually receives 40% of the Community funding as an advance.

Further payments and interim reports

For all further payments, progress or interim reports and cost statements must be submitted by the coordinator at regular intervals. The contracts usually provide for these interim reports to be submitted by the coordinator every six or twelve months. It is important for the coordinator to receive reports from the partners in good time.

For contracts with a fixed contribution (for relatively small projects or projects which are relatively close to the market and have clearly defined targets from the outset[6]) the Community contribution is paid at set dates in pre-set instalments.

Reports should be short and precise, not scientific treatises. An overview of the project from which progress can be monitored and comparison made with applications for cost reimbursements is sufficient.

Final report and final payment

At the end of the project the coordinator must present a complete final report containing the following:

▸ a full description of the work carried out, the results obtained and the conclusions;

▸ a confidential report on the possible commercial utilisation of the results and on measures taken by the project partners to protect and use the results;

---

6 For these projects the fixed contributions are paid only when the contractually agreed objectives have been achieved (see Article 7(3)(b) of the Council Decision on the rules for participating in the specific programmes).

- a summary suitable for publication (with all information taken out that comes under trade secrecy);
- final statement of costs.

As soon as these documents have been approved by the Commission the remaining contribution-usually between 10% and 30%-will be paid.

Exception: For very big projects, for which a statement of costs is required, within three months of completion of the project a consolidated statement of costs must be provided in addition to the final technical reports.

3 | NEW RULES ON THE UTILISATION AND DISSEMINATION OF RESULTS

To guarantee uniform, coordinated dissemination of research results the Council has laid down general rules in accordance with Article 130j of the EC Treaty. In certain specific programmes, however, these rules can be supplemented, tied to conditions or made subject to provisos where this is in the interests of the specific programme's targets.

The general rules aim to guarantee the legitimate business interests of all contractual partners and their rights to the utilisation and commercial exploitation of RTD results and to facilitate the use of the results in the interest of the Community.

The following general principles apply:

▶ Knowledge gained from work directly carried out by the Community or fully financed by the Community is fundamentally the property of the Community.

▶ Knowledge arising out of work as part of contracts on a cost-sharing basis is fundamentally the property of the contractual partners carrying out that work.
   NB.: Details of rights to this property must be organised between the contractual partners.

▶ Knowledge which could be put to industrial or commercial use must be suitably protected in the interests of the Community and its contractual partners, and in accordance with the respective legal provisions.

▸ The Community and its contractual partners are obliged to make use or allow use to be made of any knowledge gained, with account taken of the following:
  ● the aim of increasing international competitiveness and the economic and social cohesion of the Community;
  ● the funding of research activities for other Community policies;
  ● the agreements on scientific and technical cooperation concluded with various third countries or international organisations.

▸ The Community can allow knowledge in its possession to be used by the contractual partners or other interested parties from EU Member States and eligible third countries - possibly for a fee.

  For knowledge in their possession, the contractual partners grant licences and other rights of use on a royalty basis to one another and also, under certain circumstances laid down in the model contract, to interested third parties. The legitimate interests of the contractual partners must be protected, however.

▸ **Publication:** The Commission asks the contractual partners to publish the results of Community projects. The Commission itself publishes, after signing the contract, short summaries provided by the contractual partners during the project and on completion of the project in order to avoid confidentiality problems. It is left to the contractual partners to initiate other publications, although these must not conflict with the protection or utilisation of the knowledge gained. Details for implementing these rules are contained in the model contracts for research, technological development and demonstration.

In addition to these fundamental questions, Community research contracts cover a multitude of questions with which you should familiarise yourself. You should therefore obtain a copy of the

MODEL CONTRACT
(cost reimbursement)

**for Community activities in the field of
research and technological development**

(Fourth Framework Programme)

from the contact person for the specific programmes given in Part 4, or directly from DG XII's World Wide Web site (http://europa.eu.int/en/comm/dg12/dg12tst2.html)

It should be remembered that these provisions are not only very flexibly drafted, they are also very flexibly applied by the Commission. They are based largely on the concepts of *reasonableness* and *suitability* and permit sensible solutions to be found in each individual case. Proof of this is that no research contract has yet led to a court case.

AN OUTLINE OF
THE PROGRAMMES OF
THE FOURTH FRAMEWORK PROGRAMME

PART

The following pages contain brief descriptions of the programmes, the scheduled dates of calls for proposals and the deadlines for handing in proposals. Detailed information on areas of research, eligibility, etc. is given in the sources indicated (Official Journal of the EC, information packages).

N.B.: The dates given for calls for proposals are provisional and may change slightly. Further calls for proposals or restricted calls may be made depending on the amount of research funding available under the annual budget. Updated information on calls for proposals will be published in the Official Journal of the EC on 15 December, 15 March, 15 June and 15 September.

1. Information technologies

Council Decision: Official Journal L 334 of 22.12.1994
Duration: 23.11.1994 - 31.12.1998
EU contribution: ECU 2 035 million (including up to 12% for SME)

Aims: Development of a new information infrastructure for society and industry, building on the results to date of the European Strategic Programme for Research and Development in Information Technologies (ESPRIT).
Previous programmes: information technologies (1991-94), ESPRIT

Areas of research	Budget breakdown (%)
I Software technologies (emerging technologies, distributed information processing)	14
II. Technologies for IT components and subsystems (semiconductors, microsystems, peripherals)	25.5
III. Multimedia systems (integrated personal systems)	8
IV. Long-term research (networks of excellence, upstream RTD projects)	10
V. Focused clusters	
1. Open microprocessor systems initiative (OMI)	9
2. High-performance computing and networking (HPCN)	12.75
3. Technologies for business processes	8.75
4. Integration in manufacturing	12

Type of support: ► Shared-cost contracts
- RTD projects
- SME promotion
► Concerted actions
► **Accompanying measures** (expert networks, work and user groups, studies, demonstration projects, seminars, conferences, training, etc.)

15.12.94 (updated 15.12.95)	**Continuous submission:** open long term research, technology transfer and support actions, SME exploratory awards	**15.5.96**
15.6.95 (updated 15.12.95)	**Continuous submission:** training grants	**15.5.96**
15.12.95	**One-step evaluation:** software technologies, technologies for components and subsystems, multimedia systems, long term research, open microprocessor systems initiative, technologies for business processes	**20.3.96**
15.12.95	**Two-step evaluation:** long term research, high performance computing and networking	**30.4.96** **(2nd step)**
15.3.96	**One-step evaluation:** software technologies, technologies for components and subsystems, multimedia systems, open microprocessor systems initiative, technologies for business processes, integration in manufacturing	**19.6.96**
15.3.96	Two-step evaluation: long term research, high performance computing and networking	**16.4.96 (1st step)**

Information   Gerda COLLING
Tel: +32.2 296 85 94
Fax: +32.2 296 83 88

ESSI
Rainer ZIMMERMANN
Tel: +32.2 296 81 10
Fax: +32.2 296 83 64

European Commission
DG III/F1
IT Information Desk
Rue de la Loi 200
B-1049 Brussels
N105 8/94

e-mail   esprit@dg3.cec.be

WWW-Server   http://www.cordis.lu/esprit/home.html

Council Decision: Official Journal L 334 of 22.12.1994
Duration: 23.11.1994 - 31.12.1998
EU contribution: ECU 898 million (including up to 5% for SME)

Aims: Development of new telematics systems and services for applications of common interest. Promotion of research activities necessary for other common policies. The focus of the work will switch from data telematics to multimedia telematics.
Previous programmes: AIM, DELTA, EUROTRA, telematics systems (1990-94)

Areas of research	Budget breakdown (%)
A. Telematics for services of public interest	30.2
1. Administration	
2. Transport	
B. Telematics for knowledge	17.3
3. Telematics for research	
4. Education and training	
5. Libraries	
C. Telematics for improving employment and the quality of life	31.8
6. Urban and rural areas	
7. Health care	
8. Elderly and disabled people	
9. Exploratory action: telematics for the environment	
10. Other exploratory actions	
D. Horizontal RTD activities	15.8
11. Telematics engineering	
12. Language engineering	
13. Information engineering	
E. Support measures	4.9

"Telematics watch" and consensus development, dissemination of results and promotion of telematics, international cooperation, training.

Type of support: ► Shared-cost contracts
- RTD projects and long-term research projects
- SME promotion: exploratory awards and grant awards
► **Accompanying measures** (studies, seminars, conferences, training, etc.)

| 15.9.95 | Support actions (awareness, dissemination of results and promotion of telematics, international cooperation, education) | 15.6.98 |

Contacts

Area A **Administration:** B. O'SHEA
Tel: +32.2 296 35 51 - Fax: +32.2 296 42 60

Transport: F. KARAMITSOS
Tel: +32.2 296 34 61 - Fax: +32.2 296 23 91

Area B **Telematics for research & education and training**
L. RODRIGUEZ ROSELLO
Tel: +32.2 296 34 06 - Fax: +32.2 296 23 92

Libraries: A. ILJON (Luxembourg)
Tel: +352 43 01 3 29 23/3 2126
Fax: +352 43 01 3 35 30

Area C **Urban and rural areas:** B. O'SHEA
Tel: +32.2 296 35 51 - Fax: +32.2 296 42 60

Health care: J. LACOMBE
Tel: +32.2 296 34 61 - Fax: +32.2 296 01 81

Disabled and elderly people: E. BALLABIO
Tel: +32.2 299 02 32 - Fax: +32.2 299 02 48

Environment: W. BOCH
Tel: +32.2 295 35 91 - Fax: +32.2 296 23 91

Area D **Telematics engineering:** V. OBOZINSKI
Tel: +32.2 295 31 50 - Fax: +32.2 296 83 98

Language engineering: R. CENCIONI
Tel: +352 43 01 3 28 59 (Luxembourg)
Fax: w+352 43 01 3 49 99

Proposals Office avenue de Beaulieu 29 (BU29, 4/41),
B-1160 Brussels - Fax: +32.2 295 23 54
e-mail telematics@dg13.cec.be

European Commission **DG XIII**
Rue de la Loi 200 - B-1049 Brussels

3. Advanced Communication Technologies and Services

Council Decision: Official Journal L 222 of 26.8.1994
Duration: 27.07.1994 - 31.12.1998
EU contribution: ECU 671 million (including up to 10% for SME)

Aims: To develop advanced communication technologies and services to boost economic development and social cohesion in Europe, taking account of the rapid evolution of technology, the changing regulatory situation and opportunities to develop trans-European networks and services.
Previous programmes: RACE (Research and Development in Advanced Communications Technologies for Europe), communication technologies (1991-94)

Areas of research	Budget breakdown (%)
I. Interactive digital multimedia services	25.7
II. Photonic technologies	16.5
III. High-speed networking	11.9
IV. Mobility and personal communication networks	18.3
V. Intelligence in networks and service engineering	15.9
VI. Quality, security and safety of communications services and systems	6.8
Horizontal actions	4.9

(International cooperation, dissemination and exploitation of results, training)

Type of support: ► Shared-cost contracts
- RTD projects
- SME promotion:
► Step 1: exploratory awards for RTD projects
► Concerted actions
► **Accompanying measures** (studies, seminars, conferences, training, etc.)

There are no calls planned as at the date of
publication of this guide

Information and **Information package**	ACTS Central Office Tel: +32.2 296 34 15 Fax: +32.2 295 06 54
e-mail via INTERNET	aco@postman.dg13.cec.be *(The use of e-mail is strongly recommended)*
European Commission	**DG XIII-B/ACTS** BU9 - 4/82 Rue de la Loi 200 B-1049 Brussels

Council Decision: Official Journal L 222 of 26.8.1994
Duration: 27.07.1994 - 31.12.1998
EU contribution: ECU 1 722 million (including 15% for measures to help SME)

Aims: To promote innovative products, processes and business structures, giving proper consideration to the quality of life and to the more rational use of human and natural resources. To make small businesses more competitive. To develop new production and production design technologies.
Previous programmes: BRITE/EURAM, industrial and materials technologies (1991-94)

Areas of research	Budget breakdown (%)
I. Manufacturing technologies	**36.5**
1.1 Incorporation of new technologies into production systems	
1.2 Development of clean production technologies	
1.3 Rational management of raw materials	
1.4 Safety and reliability of production systems	
1.5 Human and organizational factors within production systems	
II. Materials and technologies for product innovation	**35.0**
2.1 Materials engineering	
2.2 New methodologies for product design and manufacture	
2.3 Reliability and quality of materials and products	
2.4 Technologies for recovering products at the end of their life cycle	
III. Technologies for means of transport	**28.5**
3.1 Vehicle design and systems integration	
3.2 Vehicle production	
3.3 Technologies to improve vehicle efficiency	
3.4 Environmental technologies	
3.5 Technologies for vehicle safety	
3.6 Technologies for vehicle operation	

Type of support:
- ► Shared-cost contracts
  - RTD projects
  - SME promotion: exploratory awards and cooperative research projects (CRAFT Community research, see page....)
- ► Thematic networks
  (max. ECU 20 000 per partner per year)
- ► Concerted actions
- ► **Accompanying measures** (studies, seminars, conferences, training, etc.)

CALL FOR PROPOSALS		DEADLINES
15.12.95	Production technologies, materials and product innovation, transport means (excluding aeronautics technologies)	**17.4.96**
15.12.94	Continuous open call for CRAFT and thematic networks: production technologies, materials and product innovation, transport	**17.12.97**
15.12.95	Accompanying and support measures (open call)	**20.5.98**

Information on RTD projects and thematic networks

Help line
Tel: +32.2 295 23 45
Fax: +32.2 295 80 46

Information on Klaus Koegler
SME promotion Tel: +32.2 295 52 90
Fax: +32.2 295 46 35

European Commission **DG XII**
Rue de la Loi 200
B-1049 Brussels

5. Standards, measurements and testing

Council Decision: Official Journal L 334 of 22.12.1994
Duration: 23.11.1994 - 31.12.1998
EU contribution: ECU 184 million (including up to 10% for SME)

Aims: To make European industry more competitive through better measurements, better definition and control of product quality. To support other Community policies. To promote research into standards and measurements and to develop a European measurement infrastructure.
Previous programmes: BCR, measurement and testing (1992-94)

Areas of research	Budget breakdown (%)
I. Measurements for quality European products	40
1.1 Measurements for research	
1.2 Measurements and testing in the industrial development phase	
1.3 Measurements and testing for production control	
1.4 Instruments of quality assurance in industry	
II. Research related to written standards and technical support to trade	35
2.1 Research to support European trade	
2.2 European measurement and testing infrastructure	
2.3 Support for customs laboratories	
III. Measurements related to the needs of society	25
3.1 Health and safety	
3.2 Methods and reference materials for environmental monitoring	
3.3 Protection of cultural heritage	
3.4 Justice system	

Applications for **grants** may be made at any time. Selections are made three times a year on 15 March, 15 June and 1 September.

Type of support
► Shared-cost contracts
  - RTD projects
  - SME promotion
► Concerted actions
► Thematic networks
  (max. ECU 10 000 per partner per year)
► **Accompanying measures** (studies, seminars, conferences, training, etc.)

15.12.94	Thematic networks	17.12.97
15.12.95	Dedicated call: CENELEC, CEN and support for Community policies	15.3.96
15.6.96	Dedicated call: CEN, ETSI, CENELEC and support for Community policies	15.11.96
15.6.96	Measurements for quality European products, standards for industry	15.11.96
15.6.97	Technical support for trade, measurements related to the needs of society	13.11.97

Contact Pierre MERIGUET
Tel: +32.2 295 42 34
Fax: +32.2 295 80 72

Information **on RTD projects and thematic networks**
Tel: +32.2 295 31 15
Fax: +32.2 295 80 72

Promotion of SMEs
Tel: +32.2 295 52 90
Fax: +32.2 299 46 35

Grants J. J. BELLIARDO
R. VERCRUYSSE
Fax: +32.2 295 80 72

European Commission **DGXII**
Rue de la Loi 200
B-1049 Brussels

6. Environment and climate

Council Decision: Official Journal L 361 of 31.12.1994
Duration: 15.12.1994 - 31.12.1998
EU contribution: ECU 566.5 million (including up to 5% for SME)

Aims: To improve the scientific base of EU environment policy: understanding the basic processes of the climate and of natural systems. To help meet the objectives of world programmes of research into global change. Development of environment-friendly products, technologies, techniques and services which meet new needs and could create new jobs.
Previous programmes: STEP/EPOCH, environment (1994-98)

Areas of research	Budget breakdown (%)
A. Research into the natural environment, environmental quality and global change	47
1. Climate change and impact on natural resources	
2. Atmospheric physics and chemistry, interaction with the biosphere and mechanisms of the impact of environmental change	
B. Environmental technologies	25
1. Instruments, techniques and methods for monitoring the environment	
2. Technologies and methods for assessing environmental risk and for protecting and rehabilitating the environment	
3. Technologies to forecast, prevent and reduce natural risks	
C. Space techniques applied to environmental monitoring and research	20.5
1. Methodological research and pilot projects	
2. Research and development work for potential future operational activities	
3. Centre for Earth Observation (CEO)	
D. Human dimensions of environmental change	7.5
1. Socio-economic causes and effects of environmental change	
2. Economic and social responses to environmental problems	
3. Integration of scientific knowledge and economic and social considerations into the framing of environmental policies	
4. Sustainable development and technological change	

15.12.95	Advanced study courses: research into the natural environment, environmental quality and global change, environmental technologies, space technology applied to Earth observation and environmental research, human dimensions of environmental change	20.3.96
15.12.95	Research training grants: research into the natural environment, environmental quality and global change, environmental technologies, space technology applied to Earth observation and environmental research, human dimensions of environmental change	20.3.96 20.8.96
17.1.95	Technology stimulation measures for SMEs	12.6.96
15.6.95	Technology stimulation measures for SMEs	27.3.97
15.3.96	Centre for Earth observation	15.6.96
17.9.96	Research into the natural environment, environmental quality and global change, environmental technologies, space technology applied to Earth observation and environmental research, human dimensions of environmental change	15.1.97

Applications for **grants** may be made at any time. Selections are made three times a year on 15 March, 15 June and 1 September.

Type of support:
▶ Shared-cost contracts
  - RTD projects
  - SME promotion
▶ Concerted actions
▶ **Accompanying measures** (studies, seminars, conferences, training, etc.)

Contacts   **Area 1:** Anver GHAZI
Tel: +32.2 295 84 45 - Fax: +32.2 296 30 24

Area 2: Peter REINIGER
Tel: +32.2 295 95 86 - Fax: +32.2 296 30 24

Area 3: Michel PAILLON
Tel: +32.2 295 41 60/5 82 87 - Fax: +32.2 296 05 88

Area 4: Andrew SORS
Tel: +32.2 295 76 59 - Fax: +32.2 296 30 24

Information   Fax: +32.2 296 30 24 or +32.2 296 05 88

European Commission   **DG XII**
Rue de la Loi 200
B-1049 Brussels

7. Marine science and technology

Council Decision: Official Journal 334 of 22.12.94
Duration: 23.11.1994 - 31.12.1998
EU contribution: ECU 243 million

Aims: New phase of the long-term strategic programme of exploration, protection and exploitation of European seas. To understand how marine systems function at basin scales, in order to prepare for sustainable use of the oceans and determine their role in global change.
Previous programmes: MAST 1989-1992, MAST II 1991-94

Areas of research	Budget breakdown (%)
I. Marine science	40
1 Marine systems research	
2 Extreme marine environments	
3 Regional seas research	
II. Strategic marine research	22.5
1. Coastal and shelf sea research	
2. Coastal engineering	
III. Marine technology	30
1. Generic technologies	
2. Advanced systems	
IV. Supporting initiatives	7

Grants: Applications may be made at any time.
Two selection dates per year: 1995: 13.02 and 17.07

Type of support: ► Shared-cost contracts
      - RTD projects
      - SME promotion
► Concerted actions
► **Accompanying measures** (studies, seminars, conferences, training, etc.)

16.4.96	Research on marine systems, extreme marine environments, coastal processes, control, forecast and management of coastal areas, coastal engineering, marine technologies	15.10.96
16.4.96	Structure and dynamics of coastal ecosystems	15.1.97

Responsible
for the programme

Jean BOISSONNAS
Tel: +32.2 295 67 87
Fax: +32.2 296 30 24

Information   Fax: +32.2 296 30 24

European Commission **DG XII**
Rue de la Loi 200
B-1049 Brussels

Council Decision: Official Journal L 361 of 31.12.1994
Duration: 15.12.1994 - 31.12.1998
EU contribution: ECU 588 million (including up to 5% for SME)

Aims: To improve our basic biological knowledge of living systems and increase productivity in respect of applications to agriculture, industry, health, nutrition and the environment. Consideration of ethical and socio-economic implications of biotechnology.
Previous programmes: BRIDGE, biotechnology (1992-94)

Areas of research	Budget breakdown (%)
I. Objectives requiring concentrated means	
Area 1: Cell factories	22
Area 2: Genome analysis	16
Area 3: Plant and animal biotechnology	24
Area 4: Cell communication in neurosciences	6
II. Objectives mainly addressed by concertation	
Area 5: Immunology, transdisease vaccinology	7
Area 6: Structural biology	10
Area 7: Prenormative research, biodiversity and social acceptance	9.5
Area 8: Infrastructures	5.5
III. Objectives treated by means of horizontal activities	
Demonstration activities in biotechnology	
Ethical, legal and social aspects (ELSA)	
Public perception	
Socio-economic impacts	

Applications for **grants** can be made at any time.

Selection meetings 1 March and 1 June 1995, 1996, 1997, 1998;
1 November 1995, 1996, 1997.

Type of support ► Shared-cost contracts
- Integrated projects Areas 1-3: ECU 1.5-5 million
  per project per year and max. ECU 100 000
  per year per contribution by individual laboratories
- RTD projects Areas 1-8: ECU 0.2-1.5 million
  per project per year
- SME promotion
- Demonstration projects

15.6.96	Genome analysis (function search and comparative analyses), plant molecular and cellular biology, somatic gene therapy, immunological substances, structure/function relationships, structural biology/electronics, in vitro pharmaco-toxicology,environmental biotechnology, infrastructures, horizontal activities	18.10.96
15.6.97	Cell factories, genome sequencing, animal mapping & selection, animal models, cell communications in neurosciences, transdisease vaccinology, structure/function relationships, biosafety, biodiversity, infrastructures, horizontal activities	September 97

► Concerted actions Areas 5-8: ECU 10 000
per partner per year
► **Accompanying measures** (studies, seminars,
conferences, training, etc.)

Responsible for the programme	Etienne MAGNIEN Tel: +32.2 295 93 47 Fax: +32.2 295 53 65
Contact	Alfredo AGUILAR Tel: +32.2 296 14 81 Fax: +32.2 295 53 65
Demonstration	Alejandro HERRERO Tel: +32.2 295 46 83 Fax: +32.2 295 53 65
Ethical, legal and social aspects	José ELIZALDE Tel: +32.2 295 72 87 Fax: +32.2 295 53 65
Grants	Alessio VASSAROTTI Tel: +32.2 295 83 09 Fax: +32.2 295 53 65
Information packages	Tel: +32.2 296 22 29 Fax: +32.2 295 53 65
European Commission	**DG XII** Rue de la Loi 200 B-1049 Brussels

8. Biomedicine and health

Council Decision: Official Journal L 361 of 31.12.1994
Duration: 15.12.1994 - 31.12.1998
EU contribution: ECU 358 million

Aims: Better understanding of the human body's basic mechanisms for maintaining health. Addressing the social aspects linked to health care. Basis for completing the European internal market in health services and for medical devices and pharmaceutical products.
Previous programmes: Medical/health research, genome analysis, biomedicine and health (1991-94)

Areas of research	Budget breakdown (%)
1. Pharmaceuticals research	11
2. Research into biomedical technology and engineering	11
3. Brain research	12
4. Research into diseases with major socio-economic impact: from basic research into clinical practice	42
4.1 Cancer research	
4.2 Research into AIDS, tuberculosis and other infectious diseases	
4.3 Research into cardiovascular diseases	
4.4 Research into chronic diseases, ageing and age-related problems	
4.5 Research into occupational and environmental health	
4.6 Research into "Orphan" illnesses	
5. Human genome research	12
6. Public health research, including health services research	10
7. Research into biomedical ethics	2
Horizontal activities: ethical, social and legal aspects, demonstration	

Type of support: ► Shared-cost contracts
- RTD projects Areas 1, 2, 3 and 5
- Basic research within thematic networks
- Demonstration projects
► Concerted actions Areas 4, 6 and 7
► Specific measures
► **Accompanying measures** (studies, seminars, conferences, training, etc.)

15.3.96	Pharmaceutical research, biomedical technology and engineering, brain research, human genome, AIDS, tuberculosis and other infectious diseases. Demonstration projects	17.6.96
15.9.96	Diseases with important socio-economical impact (cancer, cardio-vascular diseases, ageing, work-related illnesses, rare diseases), public health, biomedical ethics. Ethical, legal and social aspects (ELSA). Demonstration projects	15.12.96
Open Call	Grants in the following areas: pharmaceutical research, biomedical technology and engineering, brain research, human genome	1.4.96
Open Call	Grants in the following areas: diseases with a major socio-economical impact, public health, biomedical ethics	31.12.96

Responsible for the programme
André BAERT
Tel: +32.2 295 86 74
Fax: +32.2 295 53 65

Contact
Manuel HALLEN
Tel: +32.2 295 74 07
Fax: +32.2 295 53 65

Demonstration
Alejandro HERRERO
Tel: +32.2 295 46 83
Fax: +32.2 295 53 65

Ethical, legal and social aspects
José ELIZALDE
Tel: +32.2 295 72 87
Fax: +32.2 295 53 65

Information
Alain VANVOSSEL
Tel: +32.2 296 25 78
Fax: +32.2 295 53 65

European Commission
DG XII
Rue de la Loi 200
B-1049 Brussels

Council Decision: Official Journal L 334 of 22.12.1994
Duration: 23.11.1994 - 31.12.1998
EU contribution: ECU 646.5 million (including up to 10% for SME)

Aims: To make agricultural and fisheries undertakings more competitive by developing new methods and integrated production and processing lines. Better rural and forestry management. Health and environmental protection in fisheries and aquaculture.
Previous programmes: agricultural research, ECLAIR, FLAIR, FAR, FOREST, agricultural research (1991-94)

Areas of research	Budget breakdown (%)
Area 1: Integrated production and processing chains	15
1.1 Biomass-bioenergy chain	
1.2 Natural product-polymer chain	
1.3 Forest-wood chain	
Area 2: Scaling-up and processing methodologies	7
2.1 Chemical and physical processes	
2.2 Bioprocessing technology	
2.3 Control systems	
Area 3: Generic science and advanced technologies for nutritious foods	16
3.1 Consumer nutrition and health	
3.2 Novel and upgraded raw materials and food products	
3.3 Advanced and upgraded technologies and processes	
3.4 Generic foodstuff science	
Area 4: Agriculture, forestry and rural development	37
4.1 Reformed CAP: Optimization of methods, systems and primary production chains, agriculture-environment interactions, policy relevant economic analysis and impact assessment	
4.2 Quality policy	
4.3 Diversification	
4.4 Animal and plant health, animal welfare	
4.5 Multifunctional management of forests	
4.6 Rural development	
4.7 Complementary activities by JRC in support of DG VI	
Area 5: Fisheries and aquaculture	17
5.1 Impact of environmental factors on aquatic resources	
5.2 Ecological impact of fisheries and aquaculture	
5.3 Biology of species for optimization of aquaculture	
5.4 Socio-economic aspects of the fishing industry	
5.5 Improved methodology	
Area 6: Objectives addressed by concertation	8

CALL FOR PROPOSALS		DEADLINES
Dec. 95	R&D: integrated production and processing chains, agriculture, silviculture, rural development, fisheries and aquaculture, ethical, legal and social aspects. Demonstration: agriculture, silviculture and rural development, fisheries and aquaculture	March 96
June 96	R&D: Scaling-up & processing methodologies, generic science and advanced technologies for nutritious foods. Demonstration: integrated production & processing chains, scaling-up and processing methodologies, generic science and advanced technologies for nutritious foods	September 96
Dec. 96	R&D: integrated production and processing chains, agriculture, silviculture, rural development, fisheries and aquaculture, objectives addressed by concertation, ethical, legal and social aspects. Demonstration: all the areas	March 97
June 97	R&D: Generic science and advanced technologies for nutritious foods, agriculture, silviculture, rural development, fisheries and aquaculture	September 97

Type of support ► Shared-cost contracts, Areas 1-5
- RTD projects
- Basic research within thematic networks (max. ECU 20 000 per partner per year)
- SME promotion
- Demonstration projects
► Concerted actions Area 6
► **Accompanying measures** (studies, seminars, conferences, training, etc.)

Responsible for the programme Adelmo MOREALE - DG VI (Agriculture)
Tel: +32.2 295 96 95 - Fax: +32.2 295 12 95

Willem BRUGGE - DG XIV (Fisheries and aquaculture)
Tel: +32.2 295 51 37 - Fax: +32.2 295 78 62

Liam BRESLIN - DG XII (Agro-industry)
Tel: +32.2 295 04 77 - Fax: +32.2 296 43 22

Information Xavier GOENAGA
Tel: +32.2 296 14 34 - Fax: +32.2 296 43 22

Demonstration Alejandro HERRERO
Tel: +32.2 295 46 83 - Fax: +32.2 295 53 65

Ethical, legal and social aspects José ELIZALDE
Tel: +32.2 295 72 87 - Fax: +32.2 295 53 65

Grants Fax: +32.2 296 30 29 - Fax: +32.2 296 43 22
Fax: +32.2 295 78 62

Information packages Tel: +32.2 296 02 92   Fax: +32.2 296 43 22

European Commission **DG XII**
Rue de la Loi 200, B-1049 Brussels

11. Non-nuclear energy

Council Decision: Official Journal L 334 of 22.12.1994
Duration: 23.11.1994 - 31.12.1998
EU contribution: ECU 1 030 million (including up to 5% for SME measures)

Aims: Development and testing of safe, environment-friendly and economic energy technologies; better conversion and use of energy; greater use of renewable energy in Europe's energy supply. The programme includes research, development and demonstration measures, previously carried out separately in the JOULE and THERMIE programmes.
Previous programmes: JOULE, non-nuclear energy (1991-94), THERMIE (1990-94)

Areas of research	Budget breakdown (%)
Area 1: Research, development, demonstration and dissemination strategies	max. 5
1.1 General analysis of RTD policy options	
1.2 Socio-economic research	
1.3 Energy models	
1.4 "Energy-Environment-Economy" Forum	
1.5 Synergies between programmes	
1.6 Promotion of energy technologies	
Area 2: Rational use of energy	max. 26.4
2.1 Rational use of energy in buildings	
2.2 Rational use of energy in industry	
2.3 Energy industry and fuel cells	
2.4 Rational use of energy in transport	
Area 3: Renewable energies	max. 44
3.1 Integration of renewable energies	
3.2 Photovoltaic	
3.3 Renewable energies in buildings	
3.4 Wind energy	
3.5 Energy from biomass and waste	
3.6 Hydroelectric power	
3.7 Geothermal energy	
3.8 Energy storage and other alternatives	
Area 4: Fossil fuels	max. 27.4
4.1 Clean technologies for solid fuels	
4.2 Generic combustion	
4.3 New fuels in transport	
4.4 Hydrocarbons	
Area 5: Dissemination of energy technologies including:	max. 2.3
Activities linked to market simulation, advice on the practical application of technologies, advice and support for the appropriate application of financing instruments,etc.	

15.12.95	Demonstration - additional call on integrated quality targeted projects in the field of: 1. rational use of energy in buildings and integration of renewable energies in buildings; 2. rational use of energy in transport and urban infrastructure	15.3.96
16.1.96	R&D - additional call targeted on renewable energies (specific topics in the field of solar photovoltaic energy, wind energy and energy from biomass)	14.5.96
15.9.96	The areas of this call will be defined later	15.1.97
15.12.94	Cooperative research projects and exploratory awards for cooperative (not collaborative) research projects for SMEs	open until 17.12.97

Grants: Applications may be made at any time. Two selection dates per year: 15.05.95, 96, 97 and 15.11.95, 96, 97

See Information package!

Type of support
- ▶ Shared-cost contracts, Areas 1, 2, 3, 4
  - RTD projects (JOULE)
  - Demonstration projects - THERMIE (EU contribution max. 40% of costs)
  - SME promotion
- ▶ Concerted actions Areas 1, 5
- ▶ **Accompanying measures** (studies, seminars, conferences, training, etc.)

Responsible for the programme
Research and technological development
Michel POIREAU, DG XII-F (JOULE)
Tel: +32.2 295 15 11 - Fax: +32.2 295 06 56

Demonstration: (THERMIE)
Wiepke FOLKERTSMA, DG XVII (Energy)
Tel: +32.2 295 74 85 - Fax: +32.2 295 05 77

Information
RTD proposals
Tel: +32.2 295 58 40 - Fax: +32.2 295 06 56 or 296 42 88

Demonstration proposals
Tel: +32.2 295 74 85 - Fax: +32.2 295 05 77

Grants F. OLIVERIA-PINTO Fax: +32.2 299 49 91

European Commission Rue de la Loi 200 - B-1049 Brussels

12. Nuclear fission safety

Council Decision: Official Journal L 361 of 31.12.1994
Duration: 15.12.1994 - 31.12.1998
EU contribution: ECU 170.5 million (plus ECU 271 million from the JRC programme)

Aims: Safety of nuclear technology in all areas of electricity production through nuclear fission, in the use of radioactivity or ionizing radiation and in the presence of natural radiation. Development of a global, dynamic network to improve the identification and classification of all risks in the nuclear fuel cycle.

Areas of research	Budget breakdown (%)
Area A: Exploring innovative approaches	4.5
A.1 Conceptual safety features	
A.2 Partitioning and transmutation	
Area B: Reactor safety	30
B.1 Severe accidents	
B.2 Supplementary safety-related activities	
Area C: Radioactive waste management and disposal and decommissioning	27
C.1 Safety aspects of geological disposal	
C.2 Underground laboratories for waste disposal	
C.3 Supporting research	
C.4 Decommissioning	
Area D: Radiological impact on man and the environment	31
D.1 Understanding the mechanisms of radiation action	
D.2 Evaluation of radiation risks	
D.3 Reduction of exposure levels	
Area E: Mastering events of the past	7.5
E.1 Consequences of Chernobyl and other radiation accidents	
E.2 Cooperative networks	

Grants: Applications may be made at any time. Selection on
a case-by-case basis

Type of support
► Shared-cost contracts
  - Research and training projects
  - Support in the financing of infrastructure
    for coordinated action
► Concerted actions
► **Accompanying measures** (studies, seminars,
  conferences, training, etc.)

Responsible for the programme	**All areas except radiation protection** Werner BALZ Tel: +32.2 295 41 64 Fax: +32.2 295 49 91
	Radiation protection Jaak SINNAEVE Tel: +32.2 295 40 45/46 Fax: +32.2 296 62 56
Information	Tel: +32.2 295 40 45 Fax: +32.2 296 62 56
Grants	**Areas 2 and 3:** Christian EID Tel: +32.2 295 69 76 Fax: +32.2 295 49 91
	Area 4: Marguerite MOONS Tel: +32.2 295 52 06 Fax: +32.2 296 62 56
European Commission	**DG XII** Rue de la Loi 200 B-1049 Brussels

Council Decision: Official Journal L 331 of 21.12.1994
Duration: 08.12.1994 - 31.12.1998, (Joint Undertaking - JET - 31.12.1999)
EU contribution: ECU 846 million (plus ECU 49 million for the JRC Euratom programme)

Aims: Joint development of safe and environmentally sound prototype reactors, following on from the 2nd and 3rd framework programmes. For the period 1994-98 the priority objective is to complete the scientific and technological basis and Next Step measures for the first international thermonuclear experimental reactor (ITER-EDA). Establishment of a detailed engineering design within the framework of the international ITER agreement between Euratom, Japan, the Russian Federation and the USA.
Previous programme: controlled nuclear fusion.

Areas of research	Budget breakdown (%)
Next Step activities:	43
Construction design, establishment of reliable methods of plasma purity control. Work in the fields of superconducting magnets, operational and environmental safety, the fuel cycle and highly reliable remote handling for maintenance and decommissioning. Identification of the site for construction of the Next Step.	
Concept improvements:	24
Work in the field of plasma physics and plasma technology, and specifically studies on improved confinement regimes, magneto-hydrodynamic stability, plasma-wall interaction, fuelling and exhaust, heating and current drive. New plasma diagnostic methods.	
Long-term technology:	6
Development of tritium breeding blankets, development of radiation resistant and low activation materials, further analysis of the safety and environmental and social acceptability of fusion power.	
JET Joint Undertaking:	27
Jet is a research facility rather than a research area. It conducts research in all three areas mentioned above.	

"Next Step" activities (including JET),
concept improvement, long-term technology

Implementation framework

JET Joint Undertaking: Set up in 1978 and due to terminate on 31.12.99.
Associations: carry out work or coordinate subcontracts with institutes or educational establishments of university level. Cooperation between associations and between associations and educational establishments is to be further extended.
NET Agreement: Agreement concluded in 1983. Focus for Europe's contribution to the ITER work. Monitoring of the ITER-EDA, gathering, evaluation and dissemination of the knowledge resulting from this work.

Grants 20 grants are awarded each year - 10 each for the fusion programme and the JET. Applications may be made at any time.
Selection dates: Fusion programme: **1995:** 1 April and 15 June,
1996-98: 15 January and 15 June. **JET:** 28 February and 31 August each year

Type of support
- Shared-cost contracts
- Concerted actions
- **Accompanying measures** (seminars, conferences, training, etc.)

Contact R. SAISON
Tel: +32.2 295 40 62
Fax: +32.2 296 42 52

Grants **Fusion** - K. STEINMETZ
Tel: +32.2 295 66 51
Fax: +32.2 296 42 52

JET - J. WAGHORN
Tel: +44 1235 46 47 93
Fax: +44 1235 46 45 04

European Commission **DG XII**
Rue de la Loi 200
B-1049 Brussels

Council Decision: Official Journal L 361 of 31.12.1994
Duration: 15.12.1994 - 31.12.1998
EU contribution: ECU 256 million (including up to 5% for SME measures)

Aims: To improve the performance of European transport systems, with consideration of safety and of environmental and social acceptability and more rapid integration into the European network; support for transport initiatives in the Member States.

Areas of research	Budget breakdown (%)
1. Strategic research for a trans-European multimodal network (definition, demonstration, application)	20
2. Network optimization	
2.1 Railways	16
2.2 Integrated transport chains	7
2.3 Air transport	16
2.4 Urban transport	11
2.5 Maritime transport and inland waterways	19
2.6 Road transport	11

Type of support
► Shared-cost contracts
  - RTD projects
  - SME promotion
► Concerted actions
► **Accompanying measures** (studies, seminars, conferences, training, etc.)

15.12.95	Strategic research, rail transport, integrated transport chains, air transport, urban transport, waterway transport, road transport	**15.3.96**
15.12.96	Strategic research, rail transport, integrated transport chains, air transport, urban transport, waterway transport, road transport	**15.3.97**

Responsible for the programme   Wilhelmus BLONK, DG VII (Transport)
Tel: +32.2 296 84 55
Fax: +32.2 296 83 56

Information   Tel: +32.2 295 43 00
Fax: +32.2 295 43 49

European Commission   **DG VII**
Rue de la Loi 200
B-1049 Brussels

Council Decision: Official Journal L 361 of 31.12.1994
Duration: 15.12.1994 - 31.12.1998
EU contribution: ECU 112 million (plus ECU 35 million from the JRC programme)

Aims: To develop a shared knowledge base for the evaluation of science and technology policy options; to improve education systems and develop an education oriented society; better and more comprehensive knowledge of the social impact of European integration.
Previous programmes: FAST, SAST, SPEAR, Monitor

Areas of research	Budget breakdown (%)
I. Evaluation of science and technology policy options in Europe	48
I.1 Analysis of the RTD situation in Europe in the world context	
I.2 Evaluation of the inter-relations between short and medium-term needs and socio-economic changes and new scientific and technological developments	
I.3 Methods, tools and approaches	
II. Research on education and training	23.5
II.1 Effectiveness of policies and actions	
II.2 Methods, tools and technologies: innovation and quality in formal and informal education and training	
II.3 Education, training and economic development	
III. Research into social integration and social exclusion in Europe	28.5
III.1 Forms and processes of social exclusion and integration	
III.2 Causes of social exclusion, particularly unemployment	
III.3 Migration	
III.4 Evaluation of the impact of social integration policies	

Type of support
- ► Shared-cost contracts
  - RTD projects
  - Thematic networks (an average of up to ECU 20 000 per partner per year)
- ► Concerted actions
- ► Special measures (thematic studies, setting-up and standardization of data banks, provision of tools)
- ► **Accompanying measures** (studies, seminars, conferences, training, etc.)

6.96 or 9.96	Science and technology policy options, research into education and training, research into social integration and exclusion in Europe (only in certain areas)	**31.10.96 or later**
15.3.97	Science and technology policy options, research into education and training, research into social integration and exclusion in Europe (only in certain areas)	**15.6.97**

Responsible for the programme Jean GABOLDE
Tel: +32.2 295 67 12
Fax: +32.2 296 20 07

Contact Paraskevas CARACOSTAS
Tel: +32.2 295 08 88
Fax: +32.2 296 20 07

Information package TSER Central Office
Tel: +32.2 299 47 40
Fax: +32.2 296 21 37
e-mail: tser-secr@dg12.cec.be

European Commission **DG XII**
Rue de la Loi 200
B-1049 Brussels

Council Decision: Official Journal L 334 of 22.12.1994
Duration: 23.11.1994 - 31.12.1998
EU contribution: ECU 575 million

Aims: To add value to Community RTD activities and improve the Community's scientific and technological base through targeted cooperation beyond the EU. Better coordination of cooperation between Member States and third countries, to avoid overlaps.

The programme covers the whole of Europe, including the independent states of the former Soviet Union, the non-European industrialized countries and the developing countries.

Previous programmes: Science and Technology for Development (1987-91), Life Sciences for Developing Countries (1991-94), International and Scientific Cooperation, APAS, PECO-COPERNICUS

Areas of research	Budget breakdown (%)
A. Scientific and technological cooperation in Europe	
1. Cooperation with other fora for European scientific and technological cooperation (COST, EUREKA, international organizations)	8.5
2. Cooperation with the countries of central and eastern Europe and with the new independent states of the former Soviet Union	43
B. Cooperation with non-European industrialized countries	5.5
C. Scientific and technological cooperation with the developing countries	43
1. Sustainable management of renewable natural resources	
2. Sustainable improvement of agricultural and agro-industrial resources	
3. Health	

Type of support
- ► Shared-cost contracts
  - RTD projects
- ► Concerted actions
- ► **Accompanying measures** (studies, seminars, conferences, training, etc.)

15.2.95	Grants (Japan, Korea)	**1.3.97**
	Grants (Japan, Korea)	**1.3.98**
17.10.95	Cooperation with Central and Eastern European countries and the New Independent States	**1.3.96**
15.3.96	Scientific and technological cooperation with developing countries	**12.9.96**
15.3.97	Cooperation with Central and Eastern European countries and the New Independent States	**15.6.97**
15.3.97	Scientific and technological cooperation with developing countries	**15.9.97**

Responsible for the programme Rainer GEROLD
Tel: +32.2 295 27 16 - Fax: +32.2 296 60 20

Contacts **Cooperation between EEA and Eureka:**
Nicholas NEWMAN
Tel: +32.2 295 59 76 - Fax: +32.2 296 42 89

COST - Michel CHAPUIS
Tel: +32.2 295 41 06 - Fax: +32.2 296 42 89

Cooperation with Central and Eastern Europe and the New Independent States of the former Soviet Union:
Luigi MASSIMO
Tel: +32.2 295 66 49 - Fax: +32.2 296 33 08

Cooperation with non-European industrialized countries:
Louis BELLEMIN
Tel: +32.2 295 36 96 - Fax: +32.2 296 98 24

Scientific and technological cooperation with the developing countries:
Timothy HALL
Tel: +32.2 295 28 08 - Fax: +32.2 296 62 52

Japan grants/Korea grants:
Patrice LAGET - Fax: +32.2 296 33 08

European Commission **DG XII**
Rue de la Loi 200 - B-1049 Brussels

Council Decision: Official Journal L 361 of 31.12.1994
Duration: 15.12.1994 - 31.12.1998
EU contribution: ECU 312 million

Aims: Broad dissemination of the results of Community RTD programmes: application to innovations and transfer of technology, particularly to SMEs; support for national and regional initiatives so as to give them a trans-European dimension.
Previous programmes: VALUE (1987-91), SPRINT, Dissemination and exploitation of results (1992-94)

Areas of research	Budget breakdown (%)
A. Dissemination and exploitation of research results	46.5
1. The Community network of relay centres	
2. The information and dissemination service	
3. Protection of know-how	
4. Help with the exploitation of research results	
5. The exploitation of research and the needs of society	
B. Dissemination of technology to enterprises	48.5
1. Transnational networks providing support for the transfer and dissemination of technology	
2. An environment favouring the absorption of technologies by industry	
3. Exchanges of information and experience with regard to policies for the dissemination of technologies	
C. The financial environment for the dissemination of technology	5
1. Indirect support measures	
2. Pilot measures to promote the transfer and exploitation of technologies by SMEs	
3. Granting of technical and management assistance to public and private financial intermediaries	

Type of support
► Shared-cost contracts
► Special measures
  - Standardization measures
  - Infrastructure for dissemination and exploitation and coordination of EU Relay Centres for RTD (up to 75% of costs in 1st year, up to 66% of costs in 2nd year, up to 50% subsequently)
  - Facilitation of access to the programmes and their results
  - Dissemination activities and publications
  - Mobility of personnel

15.12.95	Promotion of management and innovation techniques	15.3.96
15.12.95	OPET - Network - Organisations for the promotion of energy technologies	15.3.96
15.12.95	European networks and services of technology transfer and innovation support	15.3.96-16.9.96
15.6.96	Financial actions	16.9.96
15.9.96	Technology transfer and technology validation projects	15.12.96
15.12.96	European networks and services of technology transfer and innovation support	16.3.97-18.9.97
end 96	Network of innovation relay centres (complementary action)	general
general	Technology transfer and technology validation projects	general

> ► **Accompanying measures** (studies, training, networking activities, etc.)
> ► Concerted actions

Responsible for the programme	Giulio GRATA Tel: +352 43 01-3 29 19 - Fax: +352 43 01-3 45 44
Contacts	**Transfer of technology and validation:** Jean-Noël DURVY Tel: +352 43 01-3 36 10 - Fax: +352 43 01-3 41 29
	Information and dissemination: Mario BELLARDINELLI Tel: +352 43 01-3 22 48 - Fax: +352 43 01-3 49 89
	Network of Innovation Relay Centres: Javier HERNANDEZ-ROS Tel: +352 43 01-3 45 33 - Fax: +352 43 01-3 41 29
	Innovation policy, regional aspects, financing, EIMS: Robin MIEGE Tel: +352 43 01-3 41 80 - Fax: +352 43 01-3 45 44
Help Desk	Fax: +352 43 01-3 20 84
European Commission	**DG XIII-D** Jean Monnet Building L-2920 Luxembourg

18. Training and mobility of researchers

Council Decision: Official Journal L 361 of 31.12.1994
Duration: 15.12.1994 - 31.12.1998
EU contribution: ECU 792 million

Aims: Qualitative and quantitative increase of the Community's scientific potential. Stimulation of training through research; improved mobility for European researchers and between universities and industry; promotion of transnational research networks; access to large-scale facilities.
Previous programmes: Stimulation (1983-88), SCIENCE (1988-92), SPES (1989-92), access to large-scale facilities (1989-92), human capital and mobility (1990-94)

Areas of research	Budget breakdown (%)
Research networks	**45**
At least 5 partners from at least 3 countries, applying common, coordinated research to a clearly defined RTD project	
Access to large-scale facilities	**15**
Admission of foreign guest researchers (EU countries and associated states) into unique research facilities where certain avenues of research are focused	
Training through research	**35**
Individual grants for researchers to spend time researching in another EU Member State	
A. Training grants (graduate and post-doctoral researchers)	
B. Return grants	
C. Grants for established researchers	
Accompanying measures	**5**
Euroconferences, summer schools and practical training courses	

Areas:

Exact, natural and engineering sciences, economic, social and human sciences that help attain the Community's research, development and demonstration objectives.

Type of support
► Shared-cost contracts (networks and large-scale facilities)
► Concerted actions (studies, seminars, etc. in the field of large-scale facilities
► Training through research: grants for graduate, post-doctoral and experienced researchers, and return assistance for researchers from disadvantaged regions
► **Accompanying measures** (Euroconferences, summer schools and practical training

15.12.95	Euroconferences, summer schools and courses for practical training	**1.4.96**
15.3.96	Grants for training through research	**17.6.96**
17.6.96	Euroconferences, summer schools and courses for practical training	**30.9.96**
16.9.96	Research networks	**3.2.97**
16.9.96	Grants for training through research	**16.12.96**
16.9.96	Access to large-scale facilities	**16.12.96**
16.12.96	Euroconferences, summer schools and courses for practical training	**1.4.97**
17.3.97	Grants for training through research	**16.6.97**
17.3.97	Access to large-scale facilities	**16.6.97**
16.6.97	Euroconferences, summer schools and courses for practical training	**30.9.97**
15.9.97	Grants for training through research	**15.12.97**
15.12.97	Euroconferences, summer schools and courses for practical training	**31.3.98**

Responsible for the programme Dreux DE NETTANCOURT
Tel: +32.2 295 40 44/5 64 91 - Fax: +32.2 295 69 95

General Information Graham BLYTHE
Tel: +32.2 295 58 22 - Fax: +32.2 296 32 70

Contacts **Networks:**
Peter KIND
Tel: +32.2 295 07 99 - Fax: +32.2 296 32 70

Access to large-scale facilities:
Marco MALACARNE
Tel: +32.2 295 52 77 - Fax: +32.2 295 69 95

Training of researchers:
Finbarr McSWEENEY
Tel: +32.2 296 50 69 - Fax: +32.2 296 32 70

Accompanying measures:
Jürgen ROSENBAUM
Tel: +32.2 296 90 28 - Fax: +32.2 296 32 70

Information Tel: +32.2 296 02 54, +32.2 295 08 43
Fax: +32.2 296 21 36, +32.2 296 21 33

European Commission **DG XII**
Rue de la Loi 200 - B-1049 Brussels

Grants under the fourth framework programme

A central concern of the fourth framework programme is to develop and make better use of human resources through the training and mobility of researchers. The specific programmes therefore offer interesting opportunities for young scientists and continued training for highly qualified science researchers. Those who receive grants are thus able to complete their training, develop a specialization or undertake research in another EU Member State.

The training grants awarded through the specific programmes complement the activities of the fourth activity "Training and Mobility of Researchers". Unlike the latter, however, they promote a top-down approach, i.e. projects must correspond to the objectives of the specific programmes of the first activity. Where this is not the case, support may be considered under the Training and Mobility of Researchers programme, which takes a bottom-up approach, i.e. topics may be chosen freely within the framework of the given areas of science.

New: In the interest of a consistent support strategy, a uniform support concept is being introduced for several specific programmes. The table below shows which programmes are included and how many grants are due to be awarded in which categories.

SPECIFIC PROGRAMMES	GRANT FUNDING ECU MILLION	NO OF GRANTS	CATEGORIES 20	30	40	R
Training and mobility of researchers	260	3000-4000	●	●	●	●
Measurement and testing	2	15-25	●	●	●	●
Environment and climate	11	60-90	●	●		●
Marine science and technology	4,5	40-60	●	●		●
Biotechnology	33	350	●	●	●	●
Biomedicine and health	17	200	●	●		
Agriculture and fisheries	30	500	●	●	●	●
Non-nuclear energy	2	25	●	●	●	
Nuclear fission safety	1	25	●	●		
Fusion and JET Joint Undertaking	6	60	●	●	●	●

Participants

Applications may be made by advanced students or by young or experienced researchers who are nationals of an EU Member State or an Associated State (Iceland, Israel, Liechtenstein, Norway). The host institute (in the EU and associated countries) must have its own research capacity.

Applicants must carry out the research work in a country other than their own. Support cannot be provided for grant holders from Associated States who wish to work in a host institute in an Associated State.

Categories of grant

The new support concept lays down four categories of grants for researchers with different levels of experience.

Training grants

Training or specialization in another country, to gain knowledge in a new field or expand one's knowledge in one's own field of expertise

Category 20   *Requirements:* university qualification or equivalent examination giving entitlement to a doctorate or equivalent qualification
Duration: 6 to 36 months

Category 30   *Requirements:* Doctorate (or equivalent qualification) or 4 years of research activity since the university degree
Age limit: 35
Duration: 6 to 24 months

Grants for experienced researchers

To support research teams in the less developed regions of another Member State (e.g. as visiting professor) or

for special training in areas of science other than one's own and carrying out experiments in science facilities or with techniques which are unavailable in one's own country

Category 40   *Requirements:* 8 years' post-doctoral research experience
Duration: 3 to 12 months

Return grants

for researchers from the less well developed regions of the Community.

Category R   *Requirements:* Doctoral qualification within the framework of a category 30 training grant
This should be an incentive to apply the newly gained knowledge in one's home region.
Duration: 6 to 12 months

Financial scope of grants

In principle, grants of categories 20, 30 and R comprise four elements:

▸ A living allowance corresponding, in net terms, to the salary usually paid by the host institute to researchers with comparable experience;
▸ Mobility allowance to compensate for the additional costs linked to the stay in the foreign country (does not apply in the case of category R return grants);
▸ Travel expenses;
▸ Contribution towards the research and administration costs of the host institute.

The Commission will determine the size of the grant for experienced researchers (category 40) on the basis of proposals from the host institute.

Application deadlines and selection dates for awarding grants are given in the information on the specific programmes in Part 4.

Important innovation: Applications for grants within the framework of the new uniform support concept are not to be sent to the individual specific programmes, but will be dealt with centrally at the following address:

Information   regarding conditions of personal eligibility
               Tel: +32.2 295 51 63
               Fax: +32.2 295 69 95

               on legal and financial aspects
               Tel: +32.2 295 19 79
               Fax: +32.2 296 99 26

Information packages   **European Commission - DG XII-G-3**
                        Rue de la Loi 200
                        B-1049 Brussels
                        Fax: +32.2 296 21 33
                               +32.2 295 69 95

European Commission   **Directorate-General XII-G-4**
                           Rue de la Loi 200
                           B-1049 Brussels

Grants for Japan and South Korea

The specific programme of Cooperation with Third Countries and International Organizations provides grants to work in Japan and South Korea in the fields of natural and engineering sciences and economic and management sciences. Applications may be made by students following post-doctoral courses and by researchers with comparable scientific experience (aged between 25 and 35). Applicants must have a good knowledge of English and already have contacts with research institutes in Japan or South Korea. More specifically, the following are available:

▶ Grants for young European researchers and engineers who wish to work in a Japanese or South Korean laboratory (university, research centre or undertaking). Maximum duration: 18 months.

▶ Pilot measures for European chairs in Japan, providing experienced lecturers and researchers with 3 to 6 months of teaching/research activity.

▶ Grants in the area of production technologies for European engineers wishing to work for between 6 and 11 months in a Japanese undertaking.

The stay in Japan is preceded by an intensive Japanese language course, normally lasting three months but which can be extended to six months where necessary.

Deadlines for applications: see page 141.

Information   Mario MERLA
European Commission - DG XII-B-3
Rue de la Loi 200
B-1049 Brussels
Fax: +32.2 296 98 24

Grants in other specific programmes

The Industrial and Materials Technologies programme offers training grants in industry to young researchers and engineers with university degrees or equivalent qualifications.

Information   Peter ROBINSON
European Commission - DG XII-C-2
Rue de la Loi 200
B-1049 Brussels
Fax: +32.2 296 05 50

Details of the conditions for grants under the specific programme on Transport will be supplied upon request.

Information   José ELIAS
European Commission - Directorate-General for Transport
Rue de la Loi 200
B-1049 Brussels
Fax: +32.2 296 83 50

The specific programme of Targeted Socio-economic Research supports training within the framework of advanced study courses.

Information   Virginia VITORINO
European Commission - DG XII-A-2
Rue de la Loi 200
B-1049 Brussels
Fax: +32.2 296 05 60

The JRC awards grants to graduate and post-doctoral researchers who wish to spend between 6 months and 2 or 3 years working in one of the JRC institutes. The scientific profile of the applicant must correspond to the JRC's areas of research.

Support is provided in accordance with the standard model for the specific programmes of the fourth framework programme. Post-doctoral researchers (category 30) and post-graduate researchers (category 20) may apply at any time.

Grants will be awarded at the discretion of the Director-General of the JRC. Applications should be sent to the science correspondents of the individual JRC institutes.

JRC science correspondents

Joint Research Centre   **Institute for Reference Materials and Measurements**
(formerly CBNM)
Achiel DERUYTTER
Steenweg op Retie
B-2440 GEEL
Tel: + 32 14 57 12 72
Fax: + 32 14 58 42 73

Joint Research Centre   **Institute for Advanced Materials**
Michael CUNDY
P.O.Box 2
NL-1755 ZG PETTEN
Tel: + 31 22 46 53 32
Fax: + 31 22 46 33 93

Joint Research Centre   **Institute for Transuranium Elements**
Jean FUGER
Postfach 23 40
D-76011 Karlsruhe
Tel: + 49 72 47 8 43 54
Fax: + 49 72 47 27 12

Joint Research Centre   **Institute for Systems Engineering and**
Information Technology
Kurt GIEGERICH
I-21020 ISPRA (VA)
Tel: + 39 332 78 55 13
Fax: + 39 332 78 98 66

Joint Research Centre   **Institute for Safety Technology**
Samuele ZANELLA
I-21020 ISPRA (VA)
Tel: + 39 332 78 97 00
Fax: + 39 332 78 99 03

Joint Research Centre   **Institute for the Environment**
Guglielmo ROSSI
I-21020 ISPRA (VA)
Tel: + 39 332 78 99 81
Fax: + 39 332 78 56 31

Joint Research Centre   **Institute for Remote-Sensing Applications**
Alan Steven BELWARD
I-21020 ISPRA (VA)
Tel: + 39 332 78 92 98
Fax: + 39 332 78 90 73

Joint Research Centre   **Institute for Prospective Technological Studies**
Carlos ARRIBAS
E-41092 SEVILLA
Tel: + 34 5448 8275
Fax: + 34 5448 8279

PART **4**

Annex

SOURCES OF INFORMATION

1. European Commission

European Commission

Rue de la Loi 200   Bâtiment Jean Monnet
B-1049 Brussels   Rue Alcide de Gasperi
Tel: +32 2 235 11 11   L-2920 Luxembourg
Telex 21877 COMEU B   Telex 3423/3446/3476 COMEUR LU

Directorates-General

DG I	External Relations: Commercial Policy and Relations with North America, the Far East, Australia and New Zealand
DG IA	External Relations: European and the New Independant Sates, External Policy and Common Security
DG IB	External relations and Cooperationn with the South Mediterranean, the Middle and Near East, Latin America, South and South-East Asia
DG II	Economic and Financial Affairs
DG III*	Industry
DG IV	Competition
DG V	Employment, Industrial Relations and Social Affairs
DG VI*	Agriculture
DG VII*	Transport
DG VIII	Development
DG IX	Personnel and Administration
DG X	Audiovisual Media, Information, Communication and Culture
DG XI	Environment, Nuclear Safety and Civil Protection
DG XII*	Science, Research and Development

DG XIII*	Telecommunications, Information Market and Exploitation of Research
DG XIV*	Fisheries
DG XV	Internal Market and Financial Services
DG XVI	Regional Policies
DG XVII*	Energy
DG XVIII	Credit and Investments
DG XIX	Budgets
DG XX	Financial Control
DG XXI	Customs and Indirect Taxation
DG XXII	Education, training and Youth
DG XXIII	Enterprise Policy, Distributive Trades, Tourism and Cooperatives
DG XXIV	Consumer Policy

* *Directorates-General which run research and technology programmes*

- European Community Humanitarian Office
- Euratom Supply Agency
- Office for Official Publications of the European Communities
- European Foundation for the Improvement of Living and Working Conditions
- European Centre for the Development of Vocational Training (Cedefop)

2. Community Offices

In alphabetical order by country in which Delegations and suboffices of the European Union are situated

Austria / Belgium / Denmark / Finland / France / Germany / Greece / Ireland / Italy / Luxembourg / Portugal / Spain / Sweden / The Netherlands / United Kingdom

A - Austria

Vienna
Europäische Kommission
Vertretung in Österreich
Hoyosgasse 5
AT-1040 Wien
Tel: +(43-1) 505 33 79
Fax: +(43-1) 505 33 79-7
Telex: (047) 133152 EUROP A

Wolfgang STREITENBERGER
Leiter der Vertretung

B - Belgium

Bruxelles/Brussel
Commission Européenne
Bureau en Belgique

Europese Commissie
Bureau in België
Rue Archimède 73 /
Archimedesstraat 73
B-1040 Bruxelles / Brussel
Tel: +(32-2) 295 38 44
Fax: +(32-2) 295 01 66

Joseph VAN DEN BROECK
Directeur

DK - Denmark

København
Europa-Kommissionen
Repræsentation i Danmark
Østergade 61 (Højbrohus)
Postbox 144
DK-1004 København K
Tel: +(45-33) 14 41 40
Fax: +(45-33) 11 12 03

Jens NYMAND CHRISTENSEN
Direktør

SF - Finland

Helsinki
Euroopan komissio
Suomen edustusto
Europeiska Kommissionen
Representation i Finland
Pohjoisesplanadi 31/Norra
esplanaden 31
PL 234/PB 234
FIN-00131 Helsinki/Helsingfors
Puh./Tel.: +(358-0) 656 420
Fax: +(358-0) 656 728

Jukka OAS
Edustuston johtaja /
Representationschef

F - France

Paris
Commission Européenne
Représentation en France
288, boulevard Saint-Germain
F-75007 Paris
Tel: +(33-1) 40 63 38 00
Fax: +(33-1) 45 56 94 17/18/19
Telex: CCE BRF 20227 1 F

Christine VERGER - *Directeur*

Marseille
Commission Européenne
Représentation à Marseille
2, rue Henri-Barbusse (CMCI)
F-13241 Marseille Cedex 01
Tel: +(33) 91 91 46 00
Fax: +(33) 91 90 98 07
Telex: (042) 402538 EURMA

Charles ANDRÉ - *Directeur*

D - Germany

Bonn
Europäische Kommission
Vertretung in der
Bundesrepublik Deutschland
Zitelmannstraße 22
D-53113 Bonn
Tel: +(49-228) 530 09-0
Fax: +(49-228) 530 09-50, 530 09-12
Telex: (041) 886648 EUROP D

Axel BUNZ - *Leiter der Vertretung*

Berlin
Europäische Kommission
Vertretung in der
Bundesrepublik Deutschland
- Vertretung in Berlin
Kurfürstendamm 102
D-10711 Berlin
Tel: +(49-30) 896 09 30
Fax: +(49-30) 892 20 59
Telex: (041) 184015 EUROP D

Eckhard JAEDTKE
Leiter der Vertretung

München
Europäische Kommission
Vertretung in der
Bundesrepublik Deutschland
- Vertretung in München
Erhardtstraße 27
D-80331 München
Tel: +(49-89) 202 10 11
Fax: +(49-89) 202 10 15
Telex: (041) 5218135

Otto HIEBER
Leiter der Vertretung

GR - Greece

Αθήνα / Athina
Επιτροπή Ευρωπαϊκή/
Europaiki Epitropi
Αντιπροσωπεια στην Ελλάδα/
Antiprosopia stin Ellada
2, Vassilissis Sofias
PO Box 11002
GR-10674 Athina
Tel: +(30-1) 725 10 00
Fax: +(30-1) 724 46 20
Telex: (0601) 219324 ECAT GR

Maria SAVVAIDES-POLYZOU
Director

IE - Ireland

Dublin
European Commission
Representation in Ireland
Jean Monnet Centre
39 Molesworth Street
Dublin 2
Ireland
Tel: +(353-1) 671 22 44
Fax: +(353-1) 671 26 57

Colm LARKIN - *Director*

I - Italy

Roma
Commissione Europea
Rappresentanza in Italia
Via Poli, 29
I-00187 Roma
Tel: +(39-6) 69 99 91
Fax: +(39-6) 679 16 58, 679 36 52

Gerardo MOMBELLI - *Direttore*

Milano
  Commissione Europea
  Ufficio di Milano
  Corso Magenta, 59
  I-20123 Milano
  Tel: +(39-2) 48 01 25 05
  Fax: +Fax (39-2) 481 85 43
  Telex: (043) 316200 EURMIL I

  Gian Pietro FONTANA RAVA
  Direttore

L - Luxembourg

Luxembourg
  Commission Européenne
  Représentation au Luxembourg
  Bâtiment Jean Monnet
  Rue Alcide De Gasperi
  L-2920 Luxembourg
  Tel: +(352) 43 01-34925
  Fax: +(352) 43 01-34433
  Telex: 3423, 3446, 3476 COMEUR LU

  Paul CERF (f.f.) - *Directeur*

P - Portugal

Lisboa
  Commissão Europeia
  Gabinete em Portugal
  Centro Europeu Jean Monnet
  Largo Jean Monnet 1-10°
  P-1200 Lisboa
  Tel: +(351-1) 350 98 00
  Fax: +(351-1) 350 98 01/02/03
  Telex: (0404) 18810 COMEUR P

  Francisco SARSFIELD CABRAL
  Director

E - Spain

Madrid
  Comisión Europea
  Representación en España
  Calle Serrano 41, 5a planta
  E-28001 Madrid
  Tel: +(34-1) 431 57 11
  Fax: +(34-1) 576 03 87, 577 29 23

  Gonzalo VELASCO GARCÍA
  El Director

Barcelona
  Comisión Europea
  Representación en Barcelona
  Av.Diagonal,407 bis, Planta 18
  E-08008 Barcelona
  Tel: +(34-3) 415 81 77 (5 lignes)
  Fax: +(34-3) 415 63 11

  Miguel ARGIMÓN - *El Director*

S - Sweden

Stockholm
  Europeiska Kommissionen
  Representation i Sverige
  Hamngatan 6, Box 7323
  S-10390 Stockholm
  Tel: +(46-8) 611 11 72
  Fax: +(46-8) 611 44 35
  Telex: (054) 134 49

  Linda STENEBERG
  Representationschef

NL - The Netherlands

Den Haag
Europese Commissie
Bureau in Nederland
Korte Vijverberg 5
2513 AB Den Haag
Nederland

Théo HUSTINX - *Direkteur*

Postal address
Postbus 30465
2500 GL Den Haag
Nederland
Tel: +(31-70) 346 93 26
Fax: +(31-70) 364 66 19
Telex: (044) 31094 EURCO NL

UK - United Kingdom

London
European Commission
Representation in the
United Kingdom
Jean Monnet House
8, Storey's Gate
London SW1 P3 AT
United Kingdom
Tel: +(44-171) 973 19 92
Fax: +(44-171) 973 19 00, 973 19 10
Telex: (051) 23208 EURUK G

Geoffrey MARTIN
Head of Representation

Belfast
European Commission
Representation in Northern
Ireland
9/15 Bedford Street
(Windsor House)
Belfast BT2 7AG
United Kingdom
Tel: +(44-1232) 24 07 08
Fax: +(44-1232) 24 82 41

Jane MORRICE
Head of Representation

Cardiff
European Commission
Representation in Wales
4 Cathedral Road
Cardiff CF1 9SG
United Kingdom
Tel: +(44-1222) 37 16 31
Fax: +(44-1222) 39 54 89

Jørgen HANSEN
Head of Representation

Edinburgh
European Commission
Representation in Scotland
9 Alva Street
Edinburgh EH2 4PH
United Kingdom
Tel: +(44-131) 225 20 58
Fax: +(44-131) 226 41 05

Kenneth MUNRO
Head of Representation

3. Innovation Relay Centres

Austria

Bureau for International Research and Technology Cooperation (BIT)
Wiedner Hauptstrasse 76
A-1040 Wien
Tel: + (43-1) 581 16 160
Fax: +(43-1) 581 16 16 16
E-mail: klamm@bit.ac.at

Mr Manfred HORVAT

Belgium

Ministère de la Région Wallonne (DGTRE)
Avenue Prince de Liège 7
B-5100 Jambes (NAMUR)
Tel: + (32-81) 32 12 69
Fax: +(32-81) 30 66 00

Mr Jean Claude DISNEUR

Technopol Brussel-Bruxelles (A.S.B.L)
Rue Gabrielle Petit 4 - Bte 12
B-1210 Bruxelles
Tel: + (32-2) 422 00 21
Fax: +(32-2) 422 00 43
E-mail: jacques.evrard@technopol.be

Mr Jacques EVRARD

IWT Brussel
Bischoffsheimlaan 25
B-1000 Brussel
Tel: +(32-2) 223 00 33
Fax: +(32-2) 223 11 81
E-mail: 100420.2670@compuserve.com

Dr. Lieve VAN WOELSEL

Denmark

Erhvervsfremme Styrelsen EuroCenter
Gregersenvej
Postbox 141
DK-2630 Taastrup
Tel: +(45-43) 50 49 02
Fax: +(45-43) 50 49 25
E-mail: snk@dit.dk

Mr Soren KIELGAST

Finland

Technology Development Centre (TEKES)
Malminkatu 34
P.O. Box 69
SF-00101 Helsinki
Tel: +(358-0) 693 67200
Fax: +(358-0) 693 67794
E-mail: matti.supponen@tekes.fi

Mr Matti SUPPONEN

France

ACTION RTDA
Centre Condorcet
162 rue A. Schweitzer
F-33600 Pessac
Tel: +(33) 56 15 11 70
Fax: +(33) 56 15 11 75

Mme Mireille DENECHAUD

ATTELOR
Hotel de Région, Place Gabriel Hocquard
B.P. 1004
F-57036 Metz Cedex 01
Tel: +(33) 87 31 81 50
Fax: +(33) 87 31 81 49

Mr Remy GREGOIRE

Bretagne Innovation
18, place de la Gare
F-35000 Rennes
Tel: +(33) 99 67 42 00
Fax: +(33) 99 67 60 22

Mr Michel KERVOAS

**Chambre Régionale de
Commerce et d'Industrie de
Rhône -Alpes (ARIST)**
75, cours Albert Thomas
6° Avenue
F-69447 Lyon Cedex 03
Tel: +(33) 72 11 43 21
Fax: +(33) 72 11 43 23
E-mail: pheyde@serveur.dtr.fr

Mr Claude SABATIN

**Chambre Régionale de
Commerce et d'Industrie de
Bourgogne (ARIST)**
68, rue Chevreul
BP 209
F-21006 Dijon
Tel: +(33) 80 63 52 66
Fax: +(33) 80 63 85 58
E-mail:
arist.bourgogne@pobox.oleane.com

Mr Ludovic DENOYELLE

**Chambre de Commerce et
d'Industrie de Paris (BRIST)**
2, rue de Viarmes
F-75040 Paris Cedex 01
Tel: +(33-1) 45 08 35 39
Fax: +(33-1) 45 08 39 79
E-mail: wur@dnsccip.ccip.fr

Mr Gilles WURMSER

**Route des Hautes
Technologies (RHT)**
Espace Colbert II
8, rue Sainte Barbe
F-13231 Marseille Cedex 01
Tel: +(33) 91 14 05 60
Fax: +(33) 91 14 05 70
E-mail: rht@rht.cr-paca.fr

Mr Christian DUBARRY

**Association Inter-Régionale
sur la Recherche Européenne
(AIRE)**
RN-25 Lieu dit Le Ramponneau
F-80260 Poulainville (Amiens)
Tel: +(33) 22 43 74 04
Fax: +(33) 22 43 72 02

Mme Nathalie GERARD

French Associate Member
**Association Nationale de la
Recherche Technique (ANRT)**
101 Avenue Raymond Poincarré
F-75166 Paris
Tel: + (33-1) 53 70 10 70
Fax: + (33-1) 47 04 25 20

Mme Françoise GIRAULT

Germany

Hessische Technologiestiftung
Abraham-Lincoln-Str. 38 - 42
D-65189 Wiesbaden
Tel: +(49-611) 774 294
Fax: +(49-611) 774 313
E-mail: volker.schucht.hlt @rs.dm.ch

Mr Volker SCHUCHT

**Agentur für
Innovationsförderung &
Technologietransfer GmbH
(Agil GmbH)**
Chamber of Commerce Leipzig
Goerdelerring 5
D-04109 Leipzig
Tel: +(49-341) 1267 480
Fax: +(49-341) 1267 464

Mr Henning PENZHOLZ

**Niedersächsische Agentur für
Technologietransfer und
Innovation GmbH (NATI)**
Vahrenwalder Str. 7
D-30165 Hannover
Tel: +(49-511) 9357 430
Fax: +(49-511) 9357 439
E-mail: nati@asysha.asys-h.de

Mr Uwe JENSEN

Zentrum für Innovation
&Technik in Nordrhein-
Westfalen GmbH
(ZENIT)
Dohne 54
D-45468 Mülheim
Tel: +(49-208) 3000 431
Fax: +(49-208) 3000 429
E-mail: wo@www.zenit.de

Mr Peter WOLFMEYER

Steinbeis-Europa-Zentrum
der Steinbeis- Stiftung
Haus der Wirtschaft
Willi-Bleicher-Str. 19
D-70174 Stuttgart
Tel: +(49-711) 1234 010
Fax: +(49-711) 1234 011
E-mail:
steinbeis_europa@s.magicvillage.de

Mrs A. LE CORRE-FRISCH

VDI/VDE Technologiezentrum
Informationstechnik GmbH
Rheinstr. 10 B
D-14513 Teltow/Berlin
Tel: +(49-3328) 435 173
Fax: +(49-3328) 435 216
E-mail: gessner@vdivde-it.de

Mr Wolfgang GESSNER

Greece

National Documentation
Centre (NHRF)
Hellenic Innovation Relay Centre
48 Vas. Konstantinou Ave
GR-11635 Athens
Tel: +(30-1) 724 9029
Fax: +(30-1) 724 6824
E-mail:
hvrc@apollon.servicenet.ariane-t.gr

Mrs Lela POULAKAKI

Forth
1414 Campus of the University
of Patras
GR-26500 Patras
Tel: +(30-61) 997 574
Fax: +(30-61) 990 328
E-mail: alkis@rea.iceht.forth.gr

Prof. Alkiviades PAYATAKES

Iceland

Icelandic Research
Council Rannis
Laugavegi 13
IS-101 Reykjavik
Tel: +(354) 562 1320
Fax: +(354) 552 9814
E-mail: valdi@rhi.hi.is

Mr Thorvald FINNBJÖRNSSON

Ireland

FORBAIRT
Irish Innovation Relay Centre
Glasnevin
IE Dublin 9
Tel: +(353-1) 808 2000
Fax: +(353-1) 808 2008
E-mail: timmonsd@forbairt.ie

Ms Dorothy TIMMONS

Italy

Camera di Commercio di Torino
Via S. Francesco da Paola 24
I-10123 Torino
Tel: +(39-11) 571 6377
Fax: +(39-11) 571 6517
E-mail: eurosp@nic.alpcom.it

Mr Pierluigi MODOTTI

Consorzio MIP Politecnico
di Milano
Via Rombon, 11
I-20134 Milano
Tel: +(39-2) 215 1500
Fax: + (39-2) 215 2309
E-mail: angelo.gatto@galactica.it

Mr Angelo GATTO

ENEA
Via Don Fiammelli
I-40100 Bologna
Tel: +(39-51) 609 8378
Fax: +(39-51) 609 8255
E-mail:
lesca@risc990.bologna.enea.it

Mr Massimo GAZZOTTI

Consorzio Pisa Ricerche
Piazza Alessandro D'Ancona, 1
I-56127 Pisa
Tel: +(39-50) 906 260
Fax: +(39-50) 540 056
E-mail:
giachetti@rebecca.pisa.ccr.it

Ms Cinzia GIACHETTI

CNR-UTIBNoT
Via Tiburtina, 770
I-00159 Roma
Tel: +(39-6) 499 32558
Fax: +(39-6) 407 5815

Ms Maria Saveria CINQUEGRANI

Tecnopolis CSATA Novus Ortus
S.P. per Casamassima Km3
I-70010 Valenzano (Ba)
Tel: +(39-80) 877 0366
Fax: +(39-80) 877 0247
E-mail: iride@vm.csata.it

Mr Francesco SURICO

Consorzio Catania Ricerche
Viale A. Doria 8
I-95125 Catania
Tel: +(39-95) 221 921
Fax: +(39-95) 339 734
E-mail: bocchieri@dipmat.unict.it

Mr Francesco CAPPELLO

**Italian Associate Member
Agenzia per la Promozione
della Richerche Europea**
Via Flaminia 43
I-00196 Roma
Tel: +(39-6) 323 2617
Fax: +(39-6) 323 2618

Mrs Roberta ZOBBI

Luxembourg

LUXINNOVATION
7, rue Alcide de Gasperi
L-1615 Luxembourg-Kirchberg
Tel: +(352) 436 263
Fax: +(352) 432 328
E-mail: serge.pommerell@sitel.lu

Mr Serge POMMERELL

Netherlands

EG-Liaison
Grote Markstraat 43
Postbus 13766
NL-2501 Et Den Haag
Tel: +(31-70) 346 7200
Fax: +(31-70) 356 2811
E-mail: avanpaas@egl.nl

Mr Adrian VAN PAASSEN

Norway

SINTEF
Strindveien 4
N-7034 Trondheim
Tel: +(47-73) 593 000
Fax: +(47-73) 592 480
E-mail: thor.o.olsen@hla.sintef.no

Mr Sven SAMUELSEN

**Norwegian Associate Member
EU ForskingsInfo**
Pb. 2700 St. Hanshaugen
Stensberggata 26
N-0131 Oslo
Tel: +(47-22) 037 000
Fax: +(47-22) 037 0001

Ms Kristin HIUGEN

Portugal

Agência de Inovaçao S.A.
Av. dos Combatentes 43-10° C/D
Edificio Greenpark
P-1600 Lisboa
Tel: +(351-1) 727 1365
Fax: +(351-1) 727 1733
E-mail: jperdigoto@adi.pt

Mr João PERDIGOTO

ISQ
Estrada Nacional 249 - Km3,
Ap. 119
Cabanas - Leiao
P-2781 Oeiras
Tel: +(351-1) 422 8100
Fax: +(351-1) 422 8120
E-mail: mcruz@isq.pt

Mr Manuel CRUZ

Spain

Universidad de Alicante OTRI
Campus de San Vicente
Apdo. de Correos 99
E-03080 Alicante
Tel: +(34-6) 590 3467
Fax: +(34-6) 590 3464
E-mail: otri@vm.cpd.ua.es

Mr José VALERO TORRES

Instituto de Fomento de Andalucía
Torneo 26
E-41002 Sevilla
Tel: +(34-5) 490 0016
Fax: +(34-5) 490 6177

Mr Antonio RAMÍREZ MEJÍAS

CETEMA
Ctra. Valencia, Km.7,300
E-28031 Madrid
Tel: +(34-1) 331 2400
Fax: +34-1) 331 5472
E-mail: cetema@fi.upm.es

Ms Teresa GONZÁLEZ

CIDEM
Ada. Diagonal, 403-3a
E-08008 Barcelona
Tel: +(34-3) 415 1114
Fax: +(34-3) 415 1991
E-mail: cidem@servicom.es

Mr Xavier DOMINGO

SPRI
Gran Via, 35,3°
E-48009 Bilbao
Tel: +(34-4) 479 7000
Fax: +(34-4) 479 7022
E-mail: miguel@gorbea.spritel.es

Mr Javier Gabilondo

FEUGA
Conga 1
Casa de la Concha
E-15704 Santiago de Compostela
Tel: +(34-8) 157 2655
Fax: +(34-8) 157 0848
E-mail: j.casares@cesga.es

Mr Manuel BALSEIRO

Sweden

IVF Göteborg
Argongatan 30
S-431 53 Mölndal (Göteborg)
Tel: +(46-31) 706 6000
Fax: +46-31) 276 130
E-mail: cb@gbg.ivf.se

Mr Christer BRAMBERGER

The Industrial & EU Liaison Office
Box 256
S-75105 Uppsala
Tel: +(46-18) 181 842
Fax: +(46-18) 181 965
E-mail: jan.jonsson@uadm.uu.se

Mr Jan JONSSON

Centek Training and Development Centre
at Lulea University of Technology
S-97187 Lulea
Tel: +(46-920) 91000
Fax: +(46-920) 99020
E-mail:owe.lindgren@centek.se

Mr. Owe LINDGREN

Swedish Associated MemberThe Swedish EC R&D Council
P.O. Box 7091
S-10387 Stockholm
Tel: +(46-8) 454 6453
Fax: +(46-8) 454 6451

Mr. Dan ANDRÉE

United Kingdom

LEDU
LEDU House
Upper Galwally
UK- Belfast BT8 4TB
Tel: +(44-1232) 491 031
Fax: +(44-1232) 691 432
E-mail:
100336.2311@compuserve.com

Mr Geoffrey Collins

Euro Info Centre Ltd. (EIC)
21 Bothwell Street
UK- Glasgow G2 6NL
Tel: +(44-141) 221 0999
Fax: +(44-141) 221 6539
E-mail:
david.cranston@scotent.co.uk

Mr David CRANSTON

The Technology Broker Ltd.
Station Road, Longstanton
UK- Cambridge CB4 5DS
Tel: +(44-1954) 261 199
Fax :+(44-1954) 260 291
E-mail: maureen@tbroker.co.uk

Ms Maureen FIRLEJ

Welsh Development Agency (WDA)
Principality House - The Friary
UK- Cardiff CF1 4AA
Tel: +(44-1222) 828 739
Fax: +(44-1222) 640 030
E-mail: 100065.3127@compuserve.com

Mr Anthony ARMITAGE

RTC North Ltd
3D Hylton Park
Wessington Way
UK- Sunderland SR5 3NR
Tel: +(44-191) 549 8299
Fax: +(44-191) 548 9313
E-mail: smb@rtcnorth.tcom.co.uk

Ms Susan BOULTON

Coventry University Enterprises Ltd (CUE)
Priory Street
UK- Coventry CV1 5FB
Tel: +(44-1203) 838 140
Fax: +(44-1203) 221 396
E-mail: MIRC@coventry.ac.uk

Mr John LATHAM

Defence & Evaluation Research Agency (DERA)
Q101 Building
UK- Farnborough GU14 6TD
Tel: +(44-1252) 392 343
Fax: +(44-1252) 393 318
E-mail: grey.wilson@dra.hmg.uk

Dr Piers GREY-WILSON

The Innovation Relay Centres are coordinated by the Commission Services in Luxembourg (DG XIII/D/3) and by the Innovation Relay centres coordination Unit. Please find below the general address and a list of contact persons within the Commission and the IRCCU:

European Commission
Directorate General XIII/D/3
Jean Monnet Building
Office C4/007
Plateau du Kirchberg
L-2920 Luxembourg
Tel: +352-4301-32950 (Secretariat)
Fax: +352-4301-34129 (Secretariat)

Internet: gaby.loutz@lux.dg13.cec.be
or X400: G=GABY; S=LOUTZ; OU1=LUX; D=DG13; P=CEC; A=RTT; C=BE

4. List of COST National Coordinators

AUSTRIA

Federal Ministry for
Science and Research
Rosengasse 26
A-1010 Wien
Tel: +43/1 531 20 71 26
Fax: +43/1 531 20 67 02
E-mail: wolte@bmwf.gv.at

Ms. Isabel Wolte

BELGIUM

Services fédéraux des
affaires scientifique,
techniques et culturelles
rue de la Science 8
B-1040 Brussels
Tel: +32/2 238 35 18
Fax: +32/2 230 59 12

Mr. Hendrik Monard

CROATIA

Faculty of Electrical
Engineering and Computing
University of Zagreb
Unska 3, CRO-41000 Zagreb
Tel: +385/1 41629606
Fax: +385/1 41611396
E-mail: z.koren@fer.hr

Mr. Zlatko Koren

CZECH REPUBLIC

Department of Science
Ministry of Education,
Youth and Sport of the
Czech Republic
Karmelitska 7
CZ-118 12 Praha 1
Tel: +42/2 519 35 11
Fax: +42/2 519 37 96
E-mail: cihlar@sgl.msmt.cz

Mr. Jaroslav Cihlar

DENMARK

Department of Research
Ministry of Education and
Research
H.C. Andersens Boulevard 40
DK-1260 Copenhagen V
Tel: +45/ 33 92 9715
Fax: +45/ 33 32 35 01

Mr. Agnette Vibholt

FINLAND

TEKES
Technology Development
Centre
Malminkatu 34 P.O.B. 69
SF-00101 Helsinki
Tel: +358/0 69 36 78 05
Fax: +358/0 69 36 77 97
E-mail: Nils.Mustelin@tekes.fi

Mr. Nils Mustelin

FRANCE

Délégation aux Affaires
Internationales
Ministère français de la
Recherche et de la Technologie
1, rue Descartes
F-75231 Paris CEDEX 05
Tel: +33/1 46 34 32 93
Fax: +33/1 46 34 34 72

Ms. Colette Joffrin

GERMANY

CHAIR
BMFT Bundesministerium für
Forschung und Technologie
Heinemannstrasse 28
D-53175 Bonn Bad Godesberg
Tel: +49/228 59 34 10
Fax: +49/228 59 36 04

Mr. Max Metzger

Bundesministerium für
Forschung und Technologie
Heinemannstrasse 28
D-53175 Bonn-Bad Godesberg
Tel: +49/228 59 31 25
Fax: +49/228 59 36 04

Mr. Stephan Roesler

GREECE

International Cooperation
Directorate
General secretariat of Research
& Technology
Messogeion Ave. 1418 5P.O. Box
14631) GR-115 10 Athens
Tel: +30/1 771 42 40
Fax: +30/1 771 41 53

Ms. Maria Christoula

HUNGARY

Department for International
relations
National Committee for
Technological Develomment
Szervita tér 8 (P.O.Box 565)
H-1052 Budapest
Tel: +36/1 117 57 82
Fax: +36/1 117 54 36
E-mail: h1586kon@ella.hu

Mr. Pàl Koncz

ICELAND

Icelandic National
Research Council
Laugavegur 13
IS-101 Reykjavik
Tel: +35/4 562 13 20
Fax: +35/4 552 98 14
E-mail: kristjank@centrum.is

Mr. Kristjan Kristjansson

IRELAND

FORBAIRT
Glasnevin
IRL Dublin 9
Tel: +353/1 837 01 01
Fax: +353/1 837 01 72

Mr. Denis Toomey

ITALY

M.U.R.S.T. Dipartimento
Relazioni Internazionali
Piazza J.F. Kennedy 20
I-00144 Roma
Tel: +39/6 59 91 26 57
Fax: +39/6 59 91 29 67

Mr. Remo Di Lisio

LUXEMBOURG

Ministère de l'Energie
Boulevard Royal 1921
L-2917 Luxembourg
Tel: +352/ 478 43 12
Fax: +352/ 478 43 11

Mr. Carlo Hastert

NETHERLANDS

Bureau EC Liaison
(PO Box 13766)
NL-2501 Den Haag
Tel: +31/70 346 72 00
Fax: +31/70 356 28 11

Ms. Leontine Frenkel

NORWAY

The Research
Council of Norway
Stensbeggata 26 (P.O. Box 2700)
St. Hanshaugen
N-0131 Oslo
Tel: +47/ 22 03 73 74
Fax: +47/ 22 03 70 01

Mr. Nils Maraas

POLAND

Komitet Badan Naukowych
(KBN)
State Committee for
Scientific Research
ul. Wspólna, 1/3
PL-00-921 Warsaw 53
Tel: +48/22 26 28 14 06
Fax: +48/22 26 28 35 34

Mr. Marek Zdanowski

PORTUGAL

JNICT - Conseil National
de la Recherche
Av. D. Carlos I, 126-2
P-1200 Lisboa
Tel: +351/1 397 90 21
Fax: +351/1 607 481

Ms. Maria Fernanda Souto
Sepulveda

SLOVAKIA

Faculty of Electrotechnics
Slovak Technical University
Ilkovicova 3 Mlynská dolina
SK-812 19 Bratislava
Tel: +42/7 72 95 02
Fax: +42/7 72 04 15
E-mail: lhudec@elf.stuba.sk

Mr. Ladislav Hudec

SLOVENIA

Ministry of Science and
Technology
Slovenska 50
SLO-61000 Ljubljana
Tel: +386/61 131 11 07
Fax: +386/61 132 41 40
E-mail: albin.babic@mzt.si

Mr. Albin Babic

SPAIN

ViceSecretariat for
International Coordination
Ministry for Science
and Education
Calle Rosario Pino, 1416, floor 6
E-28020 Madrid
Tel: +34/1 336 04 00
Fax: +34/1 336 04 35

Mr. Francisco Ferrandiz Garcia

SWEDEN

Swedish National Board for
Industrial and Technical
Development (NUTEK)
Liljeholmsvagen 32 (Box 47300)
S-11786 Stockholm
Tel: +46/8 681 91 00
Fax: +46/8 19 68 26
E-mail:
madeleine.siosteen-thiel@nutek.se

Ms. Madelaine SiosteenThiel

SWITZERLAND

Bureau de l'Intégration
EDA/EVD
Federal Office for Education
and Science
Wildhainweg 9
CH-3001 Bern
Tel: +41/31 324 48 65
Fax: +41/31 322 78 54

Ms. Ingrid Portner

TURKEY

Department of Electric
and Electronic Engineering
Middle East Technical
University
Inönü Bulvari / Balgat
TR-06531 Balgat Ankara
Tel: +90/312 210 12 58
Fax: +90/312 210 11 10

Mr. Tuncay Birand

UNITED KINGDOM

Office of Science and
Technology Cabinet Office
Albany House
8486 Petty France, Room 1/8
UK London SW1H 9ST
Tel: +44/171 271 21 02
Fax: +44/171 271 20 16
E-mail:
international.ost.ah@gnet.gov.uk

Mr. David Coates

---

5. National consultants

Since national contact points and organisations are apt to change, we have
set up a special page on the DG XII world wide web site where you can find
the latest information (DG XII's site is on the Europa server:
http://europa.eu.int/).
In addition, the information packs of the various programmes contain lists of
national contacts relevant to those programmes. The information packs can
also be retrieved via internet (the CORDIS electronic document delivery service http://www.cordis.lu)

---

6. Euro Info Centres

For up-to-date lists of Euro Info Centres, consult DG XXIII's entry on the
Europa server (http://europa.eu.int/) where the centres are listed by country.
Alternatively, write for information to:

European Commission
Directorate General XXIII
Euro Info Centres
rue de la Loi 200
B-1049 Brussels - Belgium

PART **.5**

RELATED PROGRAMMES OUTSIDE THE FRAMEWORK PROGRAMME

SOCRATES

Programme for the promotion of cooperation between universities and schools and also in adult education

Council decision: Official Journal L87 dated 20.4.1995
Duration: 1.1.1995 - 13.12.1999
EU Contribution: 850 million ECU

Content: SOCRATES combines the forerunners ERASMUS, LINGUA, ARION and EURYDICE and supplements them with measures for the promotion of European cooperation in the education sector

Activities

Chapter I: University education (ERASMUS)

Action 1:   Promotion of the European dimension in universities

A. University cooperation

within the framework of university cooperation programmes
- mobility of students
- promotion of ECTS systems (crediting of studies)
- joint development of study programmes
- mobility of lecturers to hold teaching events
- intensive teaching programmes of short duration, including summer courses outside university cooperation programmes
- study visits for the preparation of cooperation (teachers, administrative personnel, and also students where appropriate)

B. Other activities for the promotion of the European dimension
- transnational activities (inclusion of material for the promotion of understanding of the special features in other Member States; language learning as an integral component of study
- development of joint activities with, inter alia, regional administrative bodies

C. University contracts (duration: maximum 3 years)

D. University projects on subjects of joint interest

Action 2:   Mobility of students and financing ERASMUS bursaries
Foreign study visits for a minimum of 3 to
a maximum of 12 months
Maximum bursary: 5,000 ECU for 12 months

Chapter II: School education (COMENIUS)

Action 1 Partnership between school organizations

Action 2 Education of children of migrant workers and also of children of occupational travellers, of travellers and Gypsies; intercultural education

Action 3 Updating and improving the qualification of teaching personnel

Chapter III: Cross-sector measures

Action 1 Promotion of foreign language knowledge within the Community (LINGUA)

Action 2 Promotion of open teaching and tele-education

Action 3 Promotion of the exchange of information and experience, including EURYDICE (information for those responsible in the education sector of the Member States) and ARION (study visits for groups of education experts) and also other measures, such as NARIC (networks for academic recognition) and adult education

Information M. Alan SMITH
European Commission
DG XXII - Education, Training and Youth
Rue de la Loi 200
B - 1049 Bruxelles
Tel: +32 2 295 83 82
Fax: +32 2 299 41 50

LEONARDO DA VINCI

Action programme for the implementation of a vocational training policy of the European Union

Council decision: Official Journal L 340, dated 29.12.1994
Duration: 1.1.95 - 31.12.96
Funding: 620 million ECU

Content: Contribution to achieving the aims laid down in Art. 127 of the Maastricht Treaty. Improvement of the quality and innovation capability of vocational training systems, promotion of lifelong learning, measures for young people, equal opportunities for women and men etc.

Measures

Part I	Support in improving vocational training systems and measures in the Member States
Part II	Support in improving vocational training measures for companies and employees, including university/company cooperation
Part III	Support in extending language knowledge and also knowledge of vocational training and the dissemination of innovations in the vocational training area
Part IV	Associated initiatives

Implementation

The measures are implemented within the framework of transnational pilot projects and transnational placement and exchange programmes. The contribution of the Community is

▸ in the case of transnational pilot projects up to 75% of the costs with a maximum of 100,000 ECU per year/project
▸ in the case of transnational placement and exchange programmes a maximum of 5,000 ECU per beneficiary and placement or exchange

Entitled to apply are those responsible for vocational training, in particular authorities, enterprises, employers and employees, vocational training organizations and universities and also consortia made up of various supporters.

Information   M. Francis Gutmann
European Commission
DG XXII - Education, Trainng and Youth
Rue de la Loi 200
B - 1049 Bruxelles
Tel: +32 2 295 96 50
Fax: +32 2 295 57 23

TEMPUS II

Trans-European Mobility Scheme of University Students

Mobility scheme for university studies for Central and Eastern European countries

Council decision: Official Journal L 112, dated 6.5.1993
Duration: 1.7.1994 - 30.6.1998

Content: Mobility programme for universities for Central and Eastern European countries (Tempus-Phare) and also for the Republics of the former Soviet Union (Tempus-Tacis)

Supported are

Tempus-Phare

Countries entitled to support: Albania, Bulgaria, Estonia, Latvia, Lithuania, Poland, Romania, the Slovak Republic, Slovenia, the Czech Republic, Hungary

1. Joint European Projects (education projects) in which at least one university or one enterprise from a Central or Eastern European country and partners from at least two EU Member States are involved. Projects may be linked to existing networks, e.g. within the framework of the ERASMUS, COMETT and LINGUA programmes.
2. Individual mobility grants for teachers/trainers, students/trainees and administrative personnel.
3. Complementary activities such as exchanges of young people and information activities.

Tempus-Tacis

Countries entitled to support 95/96: Armenia, Azerbaijan, Georgia, Kazakhstan, Kyrgyzstan, Moldova, Mongolia, the Russian Federation, Ukraine, Uzbekistan, Belarus.

Preliminary projects (Pre-JEP) up to 50,000 ECU:
Application deadline: 28th April 1995 for 1995/96
► short visits by teaching and administrative personnel (EU to the Tacis countries and vice versa), and also further education visits for teachers from Tacis countries in the EU

Tempus II

▸ short visits within the EU for lecturers/university personnel from EU organizations for organizational or coordination purposes

▸ purchase of equipment for partner organizations in Tacis countries (fax, e-mail etc., software, books) in order to facilitate taking up contact and to prepare JEP activities

▸ administrative activities in association with the implementation of preliminary projects or the preparation of Joint European Projects

Joint European Projects (JEP) up to 1 million ECU

Application deadline: 15th April 1996 for 1996/97

Entitled to apply for 1996/97 are consortia which in 1995/96 received a grant for a preliminary project. The composition of the consortia must as a rule not be changed.

Projects must be geared to one of the following objectives:

1. Reviewing and improving university administration: introduction of new administrative procedures and structures at institutional or faculty level, e.g. student administration, financial administration etc.

2. Restructuring and development of the content of courses of studies: reviewing and developing extensive parts of curricula/courses in the priority special subjects

Information **European Foundation for Vocational Training**
Tempus Programme
Villa Gualino
Viale Settimio Severo, 65
I-10133 Turin - Italy

Deutscher Akademischer Austauschdienst
Referat 314 - Kennedyallee 50
D-53175 Bonn
Tel.: +49 228-882414
Fax: +49 228-882444

Arbeitsgemeinschaft Industrieller Forschungsvereinigungen (AIF) e.V.
Bayenthalgürtel 23
D-50968 Köln
Tel.: +49 221-3768018
Fax: +49 221-3768027

A.C.E.

Action for Cooperation in the Field of Economics

As of 1994, the ACE Programme was extended to include the Tacis partner countries. Entitled to support within the Tacis/ACE framework are: Armenia, Azerbaijan, Georgia, Kazakhstan, Kyrgyzstan, Moldova, Mongolia, the Russian Federation, Tadzhikistan, Turkmenistan, Ukraine, Uzbekistan, Belarus.

Content: The programme was started in 1990 as an initiative within the Phare[1] framework. The intention was to stimulate the exchange of economic techniques and concepts between economists in the Community and in Central and Eastern European countries. Initially valid for only Poland and Hungary, by 1994 Albania, Bulgaria, Estonia, Latvia, Lithuania, Romania, the Slovak Republic, Slovenia and the Czech Republic were included.

The research topics should be related to the process of economic reform and integration into the world economy: micro-economic liberalization and reform; macro-economic imbalances; economic integration.

Supported are

ACE-Phare
- research visits by economists and doctoral students from the above-mentioned countries to a university or research centre in the Community.
- Seminars for economists from Eastern Europe.
- Multinational networks and research projects involving at least one partner from the above-mentioned countries and two universities or research institutes in the Community.
- Attendance of economists from the abovementioned countries at economics conferences in the EU.
- Grants to Eastern European institutions offering Ph.D. and MBA programmes in economics.

1 Poland and Hungary Action for Economic Restructuring

ACE-Tacis

► Research grants: projects of a maximum duration of two years; at least one partner from a Tacis country and at least two partners from different EU Member States

► bursaries for teaching and research: economists and executives from the Tacis countries who would like to work at institutions in the EU and vice versa (maximum six months)

► bursaries for study purposes: university graduates from the Tacis countries who would like to do a doctorate at a university in the EU (maximum 30 months)

► conferences: economists and executives from the Tacis countries who would like to participate actively in a conference/workshop in the EU, and vice versa

► translations and publications: relevant works in the areas of business and management (maximum 18,000 ECU)

Information: Gerassimos THOMAS
Tel: +32 2 299 34 42
Fax: +32 2 299 35 02

European Commission - DG II,
Economic and Financial Affairs
ACE Programme
Rue de la Loi 200
B-1049 Brussels

MED-CAMPUS

Contribution of the EU: ECU 6 million
Countries entitled to participate: Egypt, Algeria, Israel, Jordan, Lebanon, Malta, Morocco, Syria, Turkey, Tunisia, Cyprus and occupied territories. The members of the Gulf Cooperation Council (GCC) and Yemen can participate as associated partners in the Med-Campus network but they receive no support from the European Union.

Content: Programme for cooperation between colleges, universities and higher professional education organizations from the Member States of the European Union and from Mediterranean countries which do not belong to the EU. The aim is to develop scientific, technical and professional capabilities.

Areas
- regional development
- social and economic development
- management of public and private enterprises
- environmental management
- cultural exchange

The programme covers the following types of activity

strengthening of contacts between the universities of the EU member states and those of non-EU mediterranean countries; regional cooperation; improvement of university structures; activities complementing other mediterranean programmes.

Information Jacques GIRAUDON
Tel: +32 2 29 562 43
Fax: +32 2 29 666 53

Med-Campus Programme
Technical Assistance Office

ALFA

América **L**atina **F**ormación **A**cadémica

Cooperation between European and Latin-American universities
Commission communication dated 10.3.1994 Official Journal???

Countries entitled to participate: EU Member States, Argentina, Bolivia, Brazil, Chile, Costa Rica, Cuba, Ecuador, El Salvador, Guatemala, Honduras, Colombia, Mexico, Nicaragua, Panama, Paraguay, Peru, Uruguay and Venezuela.

Content: Promotion of the scientific and technological cooperation of universities by training and knowledge transfer. The programme builds on the experiences of ERASMUS, COMETT, TEMPUS and MED-CAMPUS.

Sub-Programme A

▸ Structural improvement of the university system
▸ cooperation of universities and enterprises

Sub-Programme B

▸ Preparation of activities within the framework of the exchange of university graduates and students
▸ Conception of joint research projects

Priority areas

▸ Economics and social sciences: business management, public administration, economy and business law, environment, regional integration, rural development, regional and town planning, social and education policy
▸ engineering sciences
▸ medicine and health

Deadlines

April 96:	A and B and also exchange of university graduates
October 96 and April 97:	A and B, exchange of university graduates and students
October 97:	exchange of university graduates and students

Information C. FRUTUOSO-MELO
Tel: +32 2 295 14 63
Fax: +32 2 299 10 10

A. SANTAGOSTINO
Tel: +32 2 299 08 01
Fax: +32 2 299 10 80

European Commission - DG IB
External Relations
Rue de la Loi 200
B-1049 Brussels

Application forms **BAT/CEEETA**
Rue Joseph II, 36 - 4th floor
B-1040 Brussels
Tel: +32 2 219 04 53
Fax: +32 2 219 63 84

Structural Funds

On July 20, 1993, the Council of Ministers of the European Union approved six revised regulations concerning the Community's Strustural Funds, covering the period 1994-1999. For this period, the funds have a budget of ECU 141 billion (i.e. one third of the entire Community budget), which is much higher than that of the RTD framework programme. As a result, they are the preferred tool for pursuing the European Union's policy on social and economic cohesion. Research and Technological Development figures for the first time explicitly amongst the various activities of the structural funds. The companies, universities and research institutes of the supported regions must be able to carry out those activities which are essential for regional policy. In contrast to the RTD framework programme, the structural funds do not finance research projects, but rather investments contributing to regional development, e.g. technology centres, transeuropean telecommunications networks, energy grids, environmental protection measures, croos-border cooperation, and support for professional equality between men and women. In general, the support is institutional in nature, a form of aid which is explicitly excluded from the 4th Framework Programme for RTD.

- **ERDF** (European Regional Development Fund) - reduction of the development difference between the regions of the Community
- **ESF** (European Social Fund) - improvement of the employment possibilities in the Community
- **EAGGF** "Guidance" department (European Agricultural Guidance and Guarantee Fund) - co-financing national aid provisions for agriculture and development and diversification of rural areas
- **FIFG** (Financial Instrument for Fisheries Guidance) - restructuring of the fishery sector

The funds are complemented by loan-finance instruments (the European Investment Bank - EIB, New Community Instrument - NIC, the European Coal and Steel Community - ECSC, the European Atomic Energy Community - EURATOM) and the Cohesion Funds.

Eligible Regions

The Commission has defined four types of eligible region:

Objective 1   regions lagging in their developement
Objective 2   regions lagging in their industrial developement
Objective 5b   rural regions with low socio-economic development
Objective 6   regions of Sweden and Finland with a very low population density

Types of support

In contrast to the RTD framework programme, it is impossible to submit proposals directly to the Commission. The regions establish "operational programmes" comprising actions to be financed over several years. These operational programmes are then submitted to the Commission for approval.

Information   Charles WHITE
Tel. +32 2 295 53 69
Fax. +32 2 296 60 03

European Commission - DG XVI
Rue de la Loi 200
B-1049 Bruxelles

Community initiatives 1994 - 1999

Guidelines of the Commission: Official Journal C 180, dated 1.7.1994
Contribution of the EU: ECU 13.45 billion from the structural fund of the Community

The Community initiatives are specific structural policy instruments which the Commission itself suggests to the Member States in order to support actions which contribute to solving problems of particular significance for the Community.

Objective 1 Economic adaptation of regions where development is lagging behind

Objective 2 Economic adaptation of areas where industrial development is lagging behind

Objective 3 Combating long-term unemployment, professional integration of young people and inclusion of people threatened by exclusion from the labour market

Objective 4 Adaptation of employees to change in industry and production systems by preventive measures to combat unemployment

Objective 5a Adaptation of processing and marketing structures for agricultural and fishery products

Objective 5b Economic diversification of rural areas

Initiatives

INTERREG/REGEN	Cross-border cooperation
LEADER	Rural development
REGIS	Integration of the remotest regions
EMPLOYMENT	(NOW, HORIZON, YOUTHSTART) Development of human resources
ADAPT	Training measures and improving the qualification of employees
RECHAR	Economic adaptation of coal-mining areas
RESIDER	Economic adaptation of steel areas
KONVER	Economic diversification of areas dependent upon the armaments sector
RETEX	Economic diversification of areas which are heavily dependent upon the textile and clothing sector

TEXTILE and CLOTHING INDUSTRY IN PORTUGAL

SME
Support for small and medium-sized industrial and service enterprises mainly in the Aim 1 regions in adaptation to the internal market and safeguarding their international competitiveness (follow-on programme to the STRIDE, TELEMATIK and PRISMA initiatives)

URBAN
Economic development, social integration and redevelopment in urban districts

PESCA
Overcoming structural problems in coastal regions (fisheries sector)

Detailed Information
Guide to the Community Initiatives 1994-1999, first edition
Luxembourg: Office for Official Publications of the European Communities, 1994

Coal and Steel Research

**Article 55 of the treaty on the founding of the
European Coal and Steel Community of 18th April 1951**

According to Article 55 of the ECSC treaty, the European Commission must promote technical and scientific research for generating and increasing the consumption of coal and steel as well as operational safety in mining and in the steel industry. To this end, it lays down at regular intervals guidelines which are aimed at maintaining and promoting competitiveness through increasing productivity, improving product quality and developing new possible uses.

Projects from enterprises, research institutes or even individuals are supported. Applications are to be submitted in each case by 1st September for the following year.

Article 55 of the ECSC treaty also envisages a research programme in the area of medicine and health for the employees in the coal and steel industry. The research topics are specified in five-year programmes.

The ECSC treaty expires at the end of the 90s. The research activities will then be incorporated into the RTD framework programme.

Demonstration projects in the steel industry

Council communications: Official Journal C 252 dated 6.10.1990

The medium-term guidelines for ECSC pilot and demonstration projects in the steel industry envisage activities in three main areas:
- improving product quality and reducing production costs
- providing support for steel sales on traditional markets and developing new markets
- adapting production conditions to growing environmental-protection needs

Support is given to projects aimed at promoting the industrial and commercial exploitation of new, high-performance, cost-effective techniques and procedures. Projects must be of an innovative character and must require levels of investment that ensure their technical and commercial feasibility.

Special attention is paid to projects aimed at reducing production and operating costs, improving product quality, providing support for steel sales and adapting production conditions to environmental protection needs. The programme complements the Community's steel research initiatives which have the same guidelines.

Applications for support can be made before 1st October for the following financial year.

Information   Pieter ZEGERS
Tel: +32 2 295 58 45
Fax: +32 2 2296 59 87

European Commission - DG XII - C 4
(steel)
Rue de la Loi 200
B-1049 Brussels

Technical coal research

Commission communication: Official Journal C 67 dated 4.3.1994

The medium-term guidelines for technical research in the coal sector between 1994 and 1999 affect two large areas:

- mining technology (mining operation: exploration and advance working, firedamp, mine ventilation, mine air-conditioning, working procedures and techniques of coal extraction; infrastructure; modern management methods) and
- use of coal (processing, converting including metallurgical use, burning and gasification of coal).

The major aims of the programme are

- effective environmental protection and improved public awareness of the significance of coal as an energy carrier
- improvement of the competitive position of coal
- rational utilization of the resources of the Community

The degree of financial aid for projects depends on the amounts assigned in the annual budget of the ECSC. The Commission contributes up to 60% of the overall expected costs. Applications must be submitted before 1st September for the following year. For special research topics, separate calls for proposals are published in the Official Journal of the EU.

Information   J. Keith WILKINSON
Tel: +32 2 295 55 76
Fax: +32 2 299 60 16

European Commission - DG XVII/D
Rue de la Loi 200
B-1049 Brussels

Technical steel research

Commission communication: Official Journal C 252 dated 6.10.1990

The medium-term guidelines for technical steel research in the period 1991-1995 provide for activities in three main sectors:

a) improving quality and reducing production costs
b) sale of steel on its traditional markets and development of new markets
c) adapting production conditions to increasingly stringent environmental requirements

The research topics include the following:

- reduced processing times; technical reliability of plants; physical and chemical phenomena of the multi-phase system; savings in terms of raw materials, staff and energy
- ensuring optimum properties in existing products; launching products on the market which are currently still at the development stage
- better environmental monitoring techniques; development of clean technologies; upgrading of by-products and reduction of waste.

Applications for support may be submitted before September 1st for the following year. The programme is supplemented by pilot and demonstration projects for which similar guidelines apply.

Information Pieter ZEGERS
Tel: +32 2 295 58 45
Fax: +32 2 296 59 87

European Commission - DG XII - C 4
(steel)
Rue de la Loi 200
B-1049 Brussels

Medical research [ECSC]

Duration: 1988-1992
Funding: ECU 12 million

The fifth research programme "Protection of workers against dangers at the workplace in the coal mining and the iron and steel industries" began in 1988. Areas of research are occupation-related illnesses such as cancer and diseases of the respiratory system, hypakusis, diseases of the osseous and muscular system. A sixth five-year programme is planned.

Information Giorgio ARESINI
Tel: +352 43 01 - 3 22 60
Fax: +352 43 01 - 3 45 11

European Commission - DG V
Rue Alcide de Gasperi
L-2920 Luxembourg

Social research [ECSC]

Safety

Commission communication: Official Journal L 325 dated 29.12.1989
Duration: 5 YEARS
Funding: ECU 26 million

The first programme to deal with safety in the mining and the iron and steel industries began in 1989. The tasks supported relate to technical, organizational and human risk factors.

Information Bernard LEGOFF
Tel: +352 43 01 - 3 27 88
Fax: +352 43 01 - 3 45 11

European Commission - DG V
Rue Alcide de Gasperi
L-2920 Luxembourg

Health protection

Memorandum: Official Journal C 14 dated 22.01.1991
Funding: ECU 9 million

The sixth programme on industrial hygiene in mines started in 1990 and will last for at least four years. The priority objectives include the introduction of processes to limit the generation of dust and to remove dust from the ambient environment.

Information Bernard LEGOFF
Tel: +352 43 01 - 3 27 88
Fax: +352 43 01 - 3 45 11

European Commission - DG V
Rue Alcide de Gasperi
L-2920 Luxembourg

IMPACT II

Information Market Policy Actions

Market for information services

Council decision: Official Journal L 377 dated 31.12.1991
Duration: 1991 - 1995
Funding: ECU 100 million

Aim: To establish a single market in information services. IMPACT aims to stimulate and reinforce the competitiveness of European suppliers, to promote the use of advanced information services and to support joint efforts towards the coordination of the policies of individual states. With IMPACT II, the European Commission is pursuing the aim of publicizing existing standards for information coordination among developers, information suppliers and users.

Information Giorgio TREVISAN
Tel: +352 43 01 - 3 28 68
Fax: +352 43 01 - 3 49 59

European Commission
DG XIII - IMPACT Central Office
Rue Alcide de Gasperi
L-2920 Luxembourg